D0872786

The Ancient Fable

ARCADIA UNIVERSITY LIBRARY
GLENSIDE, PA 19038

Studies in Ancient Folklore and Popular Culture
William Hansen, general editor

The Ancient Fable
An Introduction

■

Niklas Holzberg
Translated by Christine Jackson-Holzberg

INDIANA
University Press
Bloomington & Indianapolis

This book is a publication of

Indiana University Press
601 North Morton Street
Bloomington, IN 47404-3797 USA

http://iupress.indiana.edu

Telephone orders   800-842-6796
Fax orders   812-855-7931
Orders by e-mail   iuporder@indiana.edu

German 2d revised edition © 2001 by Wissenschaftliche Buchgesellschaft, Darmstadt

English translation © 2002 by Indiana University Press

All rights reserved

No part of this book may be reproduced or utilized in any form or by any means, electronic or mechanical, including photocopying and recording, or by any information storage and retrieval system, without permission in writing from the publisher. The Association of American University Presses' Resolution on Permissions constitutes the only exception to this prohibition.

The paper used in this publication meets the minimum requirements of American National Standard for Information Sciences—Permanence of Paper for Printed Library Materials, ANSI Z39.48-1984.

Manufactured in the United States of America

Library of Congress Cataloging-in-Publication Data

Holzberg, Niklas.
   [Antike Fabel. English]
   The ancient fable : an introduction / Niklas Holzberg ; Translated by Christine Jackson-Holzberg.
        p. cm. — (Studies in ancient folklore and popular culture)
   Includes bibliographical references and index.
   ISBN 0-253-34146-9 (cloth : alk. paper) — ISBN 0-253-21548-X (alk. paper)
   1. Fables, Classical—History and criticism.   I. Title. II. Series.
   PA3032 .H65 2002
   398.2'0938—dc21
                                    2002004354

1   2   3   4   5   07   06   05   04   03   02

PA
3032
.H65
2002

For Daniel Mackay Holzberg

Contents

■

Abbreviations / ix

The Fables and Their Scholars   1

1

The Fable as Exemplum in Poetry and Prose   11
    Greek Literature   11
        The Archaic and Classical Periods   11
        The Hellenistic Fable *Repertorium*   22
        The Imperial Age   25
    Roman Literature   31

2

Fable Books in Verse   39
    Phaedrus, *Fabulae Aesopiae*   39
    Babrius, *Mythiambi Aesopei*   52
    Avianus, *Fabulae*   62

3

Fable Books in Prose   72
    "The Life and Fables of Aesop"   72
        "The Life of Aesop": The *Aesop Romance*   76
        "The Fables of Aesop": The *Collectio Augustana*   84
    Aesopus Latinus   95

References / 105
General Index / 123
Index Locorum / 127

ABBREVIATIONS

Modern editions and literature on the ancient fable are cited by the editor's or author's name and the year of publication; full bibliographical details can be found in the references. The following abbreviations are used for ancient fables and related texts:

Aes.   Fable in Perry, *Aesopica* (1952)
CFA   Hausrath, *Corpus Fabularum Aesopicarum* (1940–1956)
Test.   *Testimonia ueterum de Aesopo fabulisque Aesopiis* in Perry, *Aesopica* (1952)
Th.   Thiele, *Der lateinische Äsop des Romulus* (1910)

Translations of Greek and Latin are in many cases quoted from editions in the Loeb Classical Library.

The Ancient Fable

The Fables and Their Scholars

■ Travelers in the antique land of the genre *fable* will find themselves confronted not perhaps by a wreck of Ozymandian proportions, but still with a sizable selection of rubble. What lies in ruins here is not only the classicists' approach to this narrative form—a state of decay not wholly surprising, given that the majority of scholars continue to devote most of their energies to texts which more manifestly exemplify the old Winckelmann vision of "noble simplicity and quiet grandeur." No, even the actual fables, viewed in their entirety, present a chaotic sight. The main explanation for this is that the fable was not regarded in antiquity as a literary genre per se, but was primarily used in poetry and prose as exemplum with which to illustrate all manner of observations. Books of fables did exist, and amongst those who compiled and created them were authors with genuine literary aspirations, at least when a poet was at work. However, the ancient literary scene took little note of such offerings, with the result that, in some cases, we do not even know the name of the fabulist. The books, with the sole exception of Avianus's little collection, were not destined to survive unscathed either: later editors and copyists snipped here and added on there, arbitrarily altered the order of the texts, turned verse fables into prose, and adapted the diction of prose fables to suit contemporary usage, or even to reflect contemporary attitudes. And what was there to stop them from doing all this? After all, fables were not regarded as the fruits of literary exertions, but simply as utility texts.

Fables inserted into prose or poetry for the purpose of illustration can be traced in ancient literature from the late eighth century B.C. through to the end of antiquity. Such exemplary tales are either told in the form of a structured narrative—for instance, "Town Mouse and Country Mouse" in Horace (*Satires* 2.6.79–117)—or their contents are merely outlined, often in indirect speech—for example, "The Dancing Fish" in Herodotus (1.141). Sometimes we find simply an allusion to a fable in a figure of speech, such as "deterrent tracks" and "borrowed plumes" (Plato, *Alcibiades* (1) 123A; Horace, *Epistles* 1.3.19–20). Citations of this type—direct or indirect—are of great significance for this ancient genre's history, and well over one hundred have been recorded so far. To these can be added the substantial number of texts adapted by rhetoricians for teaching purposes, most important, the sixteen fables of Ps.-Dositheus (early third century A.D.) and the forty fables of Aphthonius (fourth/fifth century A.D.).

This group—fables, or allusions to such, found in writings other than the actual fable books—is particularly difficult to gauge. The texts have never been collected in a complete edition that can satisfy modern critical expectations, nor have they ever been listed together in any accessible catalog. We do have two inventories of ancient fables: the appendix in B. E. Perry's Loeb edition of Babrius and Phaedrus (1965), and the third volume of F. Rodríguez Adrados's *Historia de la fábula greco-latina* (1979–1987). However, Perry's catalog takes insufficient note of the parallel tradition running alongside the fable-book texts, and Adrados's "Inventario" is, in its present form, not easy to use. It lacks any kind of index and poses for some readers perhaps a certain language barrier; it was in any case intended not so much as a catalog of fables, but rather as "documentación" for the ideas presented in the preceding two volumes, where Adrados tries to reconstruct the history of ancient fable books. Fortunately, a revised edition of this monumental work is in the process of being published (1999a ff.), updated, and translated into English under the auspices of Adrados and G.-J. van Dijk. The third volume is to provide a new, comprehensive catalog of ancient fables, and, since van Dijk's own book on the genre (1997)—devoted to fables appearing within literary contexts in Greek literature from earliest to Hellenistic times—has prepared much ground for such a register, there is a good chance that this will be the inventory of Greek and Roman fable material which modern research badly needs. Those unable to wait, however, must instead laboriously compile their own lists, combing the two catalogs just mentioned, then hunting through the various editions of fable books with their scattered notes on such items (Crusius 1897, *CFA*, Guaglianone 1969, also Luzzatto and La Penna 1986 are especially useful in this respect). Even then, of course, there can be no guarantee that the list will be exhaustive.

Turning now to the ancient fable books intended by their authors as literary works, we can list the following extant texts:

1. Verse fable books
a) Phaedrus, *Fabulae Aesopiae* (first half of the first century A.D.):
Latin fables in iambic senarii, divided into five *libri* that have survived in extracts only, with a total of 94 fables. To these can be added 32 fables included, without any indication of their original positions in the *libri*, by the humanist Niccolò Perotti in his anthology of Phaedrus (= the *Appendix Perottina*), 11 prose versions of now-lost Phaedriana in the *Ademar Codex*, and prose adaptations of lost fables (their exact number can no longer be ascertained) in the *Aesopus Latinus* (see below 2.b).
b) Babrius, Μυθίαμβοι Αἰσώπειοι (*Fables in Iambics*; before the start of the third century A.D.):
Greek fables in choliambic meter, ordered alphabetically in the manuscripts, that is, according to the first letter of the first word in each text (one exception: *POxy. 1249*); the extant version with the most fables, the *Codex Athous*, contains 123 texts divided into two books (reaching the letter *O*), and a further 21 (more or less in their entirety) survive in other manuscripts; to these can be added prose paraphrases—probably Byzantine in origin—of lost Babriana, but their exact number is impossible to determine.
c) Avianus, *Fabulae* (turn of the fourth to the fifth century A.D.): 42 Latin fables in elegiac couplets.

2. Prose fable books (authors unknown)
a) "The Life and Fables of Aesop" (second/third century A.D.):
A (lost) book consisting of a fictional biography of Aesop and

a collection of Greek fables in alphabetical order (according to the first letter of the first word in each); the fables survive in a form known as the *Collectio Augustana*, named after the manuscript through which scholars first became acquainted with the book: *Codex Monacensis gr. 564* (formerly kept in Augsburg [Augusta Vindelicorum] and now in Munich). The oldest manuscripts indicate that it originally contained 231 fables (plus a further 13, which are, however, only found in *recensio Ia* of the collection), but some of these could quite conceivably have been added later. And it is similarly conceivable that the two Byzantine adaptations of the *Augustana*—the *Collectio Vindobonensis* (named after the Vienna *Codex Vindob. gr. hist. 130*) and the collection of Maximus Planudes (*Collectio Accursiana*, after the *editio princeps* of ca. 1479)—have preserved, in versions not written until late antiquity or medieval times, ancient fables which are not included in the *Collectio Augustana*, but which could have formed part of it before the oldest surviving manuscript was compiled.

b) *Aesopus Latinus* (fourth century A.D.):

Latin fables which are probably all prose adaptations of Phaedriana and which, in the lost original version, were divided into five books, with a prefatory letter from "Aesopus" to "Rufus." Fifty-six of these fables can be found in the five *libri* of the Wolfenbüttel *Codex Gud. lat. 148* (formerly in Wissembourg, Alsace, hence the name *Wissembourg Codex*). These and a further 12 are in the four *libri* of a collection in which the "Aesopus" letter is preceded by another epistle; there one "Romulus" tells a "Tiberinus" that he, "Romulus," has translated the Greek "Aesopus." This collection survives in two *recensiones*, the *Gallicana* and the *vetus*, and contains, in addition to the 68 prose Phaedriana versions, 13 fables taken from other authors. Twenty-nine of the *Aesopus Latinus* fables are also found in the Leiden *Cod. Voss. lat. 8° no. 15* (= the *Ademar Codex*, after its copyist), combined there with 30 prose paraphrases of Phaedriana and 8 fables of unknown origin.

This survey shows how fragmentary our knowledge is of the fable books written or compiled by ancient authors. It is, then, hardly surprising that fable scholars in the second half of the nineteenth century and the first half of the twentieth—for classical studies the age of historicism—focused chiefly on the sources and the original contents and structure of the fable books. Until quite recently, in fact, work on the ancient fable has been confined to the attempts of various scholars to reconstruct the history of the collections. These began in 1894 with A. Hausrath's first examination of the subject, *Untersuchungen zur Überlieferung der äsopischen Fabeln,* and the same approach was still being taken in F. Rodríguez Adrados's *Historia de la fábula greco-latina,* published in three volumes between 1979 and 1987. However, the most significant outcome of such efforts is not actually the development of theories regarding the sources and earlier versions of the extant texts; our consideration of the fable books will demonstrate briefly in each case that much flirting with pure speculation has been involved here. No, the real fruits of these studies are the editions we now have today of all the fable books in question, editions which satisfy the requirements of modern textual criticism. But of these, it must be said, only one can rightly be called an outstanding achievement in the field of editing: the Babrius text prepared by Luzzatto and La Penna (1986), which is based on what was in its day also unmatched among critical fable editions, O. Crusius's Babrius (1897). Even so, A. Guaglianone's *Phaedrus* (1969), his *Avianus* (1958), and G. Thiele's *Aesopus Latinus* (1910) do represent a great leap forward in comparison with the preceding editions.

Anyone wishing to work on the *Collectio Augustana* will be able to choose between three texts that are each founded on a particularly thorough analysis of the manuscripts. There exists, however, no single standard edition. One reason for this is that, given the special circumstances of the *Collectio Augustana*'s manuscript tradition, editors are obliged to include, in addition to the fables from the ancient collection, those from the two Byzantine collections derived from it. Another reason is the differing evaluation of the manuscripts reached by the three editors looking at the three versions—E. Chambry, A. Hausrath, and B. E. Perry. The result of such divergence is that each of the editions has one particular merit and is in that respect superior to the other two. All three are therefore indispensable when a close study is to be made of this 'Aesopus Graecus.'

1. Chambry (1925), whose edition includes the fables from the *recensio Vindobonensis* and the *Accursiana* alongside those of the *Augustana*, did make some mistakes when differentiating between the three manuscript groups, but, in contrast to the other two editors, he conscientiously recorded all textual variants in the manuscripts within each group. We may assume that not all such variants were simply the result of a copyist's ignorance, and that they in fact frequently represented a deliberate change made to the original wording by someone adapting the text. This means that there is a rich harvest to be obtained here by scholars primarily interested in thematic variations; for them the Chambry edition is the only serviceable one.

2. Hausrath (1940–56), who, like Chambry, edited the fables from all three *recensiones,* does not offer a totally reliable text for the *Augustana* group, because he failed to recognize the importance of one particular manuscript, the *Codex Cryptoferratensis,* which disappeared at the end of the eighteenth century and resurfaced in 1928 in New York. However, his edition of the fables from the two other groups is a vast improvement on Chambry's text. Hausrath's critical apparatus, on the other hand, is incomplete and contains numerous errors; users ought therefore always to compare it with Chambry's and Perry's apparatuses (admittedly quite a chore, considering that Hausrath, inveterately German and disparaging as he was of his French and American colleagues' work, had, for example, no qualms about using his own manuscript sigla).

3. Perry (1952) offers an excellent, critically up-to-the-minute edition of the 231 fables of the *Augustana* (= nos. 1–231 of his *Aesopica*) and of the 13 fables from *recensio Ia* (= *Aes.* 232–244). However, he leaves aside the parallel texts from the *recensio Vindobonensis* and the *Accursiana,* editing only those fables from these two that have no corresponding version in the *Augustana* text (= *Aes.* 245–273).

On the whole, then, those who can read ancient fables in the original Greek and Latin need feel no want of adequate editions. Readers who have to rely on translations are also quite well provided for in various languages. No complete English translation of all Greek prose fables has been published as yet, but the *Collectio*

Augustana texts can be found in L. W. Daly's translation (1961a), and a small selection of them in Hansen (1998), 259–271; Penguin Classics offers the 'Aesopus Graecus' as edited by Chambry (1925) in a translation by Temple and Temple (1998). The fable books of Phaedrus, Babrius, and Avianus are available in the Loeb Classical Library, translated by Perry (1965) and by Duff and Duff (1934). William Caxton published his English *Aesopus Latinus* in 1484, but there seems to be no modern English translation of the book; J. Irmscher (1978) offers a German version of all the fables in Thiele's edition (1910).

Both in the translations and in the literature on the genre, Greek fables are still frequently cited according to their numbers in K. Halm's edition (1852), and this alone ought to illustrate the sorry state of affairs in present studies on the ancient fable. True, his little Teubner volume is of convenient proportions, the alpha-betical arrangement of the texts according to their titles does undeniably make it much easier to find any particular fable, and the editor did unfailingly print all the Greek Aesopica he could find, even including many that were passed down in sources other than the fable books. But he took his texts from earlier editions instead of turning directly to the manuscripts themselves. In one very important case, the *Codex Monacensis gr. 564,* he would not actually have had very far to go, being himself the director of the Munich library where it was kept. And yet, for the fables contained in this manuscript—in his edition they represent the *recensio Augustana*—Halm chose instead to use J. G. Schneider's *editio princeps* of 1812. Schneider, however, had not actually edited the Munich codex itself, but merely a copy written in the eighteenth century by Ernestine Reiske, the wife of Lessing's friend J. J. Reiske. Again, the genre *ancient fable* truly does present a chaotic sight, but one important step toward clearing up the mess would be to stop referring to Halm—a practice which, here at least, will be strictly avoided.

One of the reasons why classicists have so rarely made the ancient fable the subject of their research is perhaps that no satis-factory study of the genre in all its breadth has ever been forth-coming. The four existing longer monographs—Hausrath's *Pauly-Wissowa* articles (1909 and 1938; S. Josifović's supplement [1974] is of little use, teeming as it is with mistakes and naïveté that are partly due to his poor knowledge of the relevant literature), and the substantial books by M. Nøjgaard (1964–67), F. Rodríguez Adrados (1979–87), and S. Jedrkiewicz (1989)—can really only be appreciated by readers who have already delved quite deeply into the subject themselves. These scholars each devote their books to one particular theory dear to their respective hearts and, as a result, tend to forget that a wider audience, one with a more general interest in literature, might require a clearer, more systematic presentation of facts and ideas. However, there are three works—comprehensive in outline—which, although they too concentrate on specific aspects, do so in a powerfully stimulating way, and it is these that can be recommended as preliminary reading.

1. O. Crusius (1913) was the first to raise questions regarding the political, social, and economic conditions that fostered the genre *fable*. His answers may be, as we shall see, overly one-sided, but the article as such encouraged numerous scholars—classicists and others—to take a closer look at the problem.
2. B. E. Perry (1959) probably represents the most convincing attempt made so far to define the genre.
3. K. Grubmüller (1977, 48–67) offers a brilliant overview of the genre's ancient history.

The first two of these are unquestionably eclipsed in terms of scholarly achievement by the third, which is the work not of a classicist, but of someone whose special field is German literature. This says a lot about the present state of research on the ancient fable, and it is even more significant that Grubmüller is the only one of the three who considers it necessary, in a survey of the most important issues for students of the ancient fable, to address the subject of *text interpretation*. What is really disturbing, however, is the fact that he can only cite one classicist who focuses not on the sources and earlier versions of the extant Greek and Roman fables, but on the texts themselves: M. Nøjgaard.

This Danish scholar's monograph was named above among the books on the genre which make difficult reading for those not equipped with the necessary specialized knowledge. And the two sizable volumes of Nøjgaard's *La fable antique* are indeed conspicuously representative of this category. The author's central aim is to provide a painstaking structural analysis of the fables in the *Collectio Augustana* and of the verse fable books of Phaedrus and Babrius. His train of thought is in most cases extremely theoretical, almost in the style of a philosophical treatise, and it is presented with the help of an intricate and confusing web of highly sophisticated terminology. This method of approach frequently causes him to lose sight of the wood for trees: only a few fables are lucky enough to be interpreted in one whole piece (e.g., "The Wolf and the Lamb" [*Aes.* 155; Phaedrus 1.1; Babrius 89] in 2:12–14, or "The Lion and the Stag" [Babrius 95] in 2:322–326). Even the most benevolent readers need considerable patience to work their way through Nøjgaard's one thousand pages of abstractions, and more than a few fable scholars certainly seem to have thrown in the towel. Except in the books of Rodríguez Adrados and Jedrkiewicz (who are, however, almost wholly committed to the principles of historistic readings), work on the ancient fable published after 1967 shows few signs of Nøjgaard's book having been used, much less of any form of grappling with his theories. Indeed, the majority of reviewers made no attempt to disguise the fact that reading the book had not afforded them much pleasure.

This is very regrettable, because there is one thing that must be stressed quite clearly here: of all scholars who have worked on ancient fables, Nøjgaard is the only one to have properly appreciated the literary qualities of these texts. He is, moreover, one of the few classicists who have made any attempt to approach Greek and Roman narrative literature as *literature* and to apply to it modern methods of interpretation, rather than just using it as a sort of gymnasium for source-fixated speculation training. And, more specifically, the chapter in which Nøjgaard presents his penetrating analysis of the fables in the *Collectio Augustana* is one of the best pieces of hermeneutic writing produced yet by the relatively small band of classicists who have shown an interest in ancient narrative texts.

It is, therefore, principally Nøjgaard's findings that form the starting point for the following introduction to the ancient fable. The main intentions here are to acquaint readers with the texts themselves and to demonstrate—albeit with a great deal less scholarliness than Nøjgaard—that the artistry with which Greek and Roman fabulists reshaped the material and motifs provided by Aesopic tradition merits the same attention as the story-telling talent displayed by the authors of the 'classical' texts of narrative literature. An introduction obviously cannot be expected to offer a series of individual text interpretations, but the literary history that a book of this kind certainly must provide ought ideally to be combined with examples of textual analysis. In the following, then, the ancient fable is to be considered in terms of its generic history and its literary form and structure. The discussion of the genre's development is based primarily on Perry's very cogent line of thought.

Otto Crusius, a student of Erwin Rohde, and as much a pioneer of studies on the ancient fable as his professor was of research on the ancient novel, named one good reason why the lesser forms of ancient narrative must be deemed worthy of thorough investigation. In his review of Hausrath's above-mentioned first work of 1894 (in *Wochenschrift für Klassische Philologie* 12 [1895]: 169–173), Crusius noted briefly and to the point: "Novellas and fables play in world literature a role comparable to that of grain in world commerce." One of the main purposes of this introduction to the field of ancient fable is to confront today's classicists with the simple truth of this remark.

1

The Fable as Exemplum in Poetry and Prose

■ **Greek Literature**

THE ARCHAIC AND CLASSICAL PERIODS

The earliest surviving evidence that the fable was in any sense formally discussed by ancient theorists is found in the *Rhetoric* of Aristotle (384–322 B.C.). In chapter 20 of book 2 (1393a23–1394a18) the philosopher discusses the two types of proofs commonly used in rhetorical reasoning: example (παράδειγμα) and enthymeme (ἐνθύμημα). For the former he names two kinds: the recounting of an actual event and the fictional narrative; under the latter he then lists two narrative forms: comparison (παραβολή) and fable (λόγος). In order to illustrate the use of fables in rhetorical argumentation, Aristotle relates briefly how the lyric poet Stesichorus (ca. 600 B.C.) and the fabulist Aesop (first half of the sixth century B.C.; see below, p. 15) both tried, the one in Himera, the other on Samos, to influence a public body in its decision by telling a λόγος that could be applied to the case in question.

For the Greek fable—as far as its history is still at all discernible today—this passage from Aristotle marks the first significant caesura, since the next, that is, the second oldest mention of the genre, records the publication by the statesman and philosopher Demetrius of Phalerum (ca. 350–280 B.C.) of a book-roll containing Aesopic fables. As we shall see later (infra, pp. 22 ff.), this was very probably the first fable book of Greco-Roman times. Aristotle's remarks on the exemplifying function of fables can therefore be placed at the end of the first stage in the development of this narrative form, a phase in which it was used solely as means to an end, that is, as an exemplum within a given literary context, for instance in rhetorical argumentation.

From this first phase in the genre's history we have, in addition to the two λόγοι cited by Aristotle, various other complete fable texts and references to such. These are small in number, and, as they can provide fundamental insights into the genre's origins and into some of its typical features, a brief survey of the passages in question seems appropriate here.

1. Fables and fable fragments

Hesiod (ca. 700), *Works and Days* 202–212: "The Nightingale and the Hawk" (= *Aes.* 4a).

Archilochus (ca. 650), *Epodes* frag. 172–181 West: "The Eagle and the Fox" (~ *Aes.* 1); frag. 185–187 West: "The Ape and the Fox" (~ *Aes.* 81).

Semonides (seventh century), *Iambics* frag. 8 and 9 West: ? "The Heron and the Buzzard" (= *Aes.* 443); frag. 13 West: ? "The Eagle and the Dung Beetle" (~ *Aes.* 3).

[Anonymous], *Scolion* 9 (late sixth/early fifth century) = frag. 892 Page: "The Snake and the Crab" (~ *Aes.* 196).

Aeschylus (525/524–456), *Myrmidones* frag. 139 Radt: "The Wounded Eagle" (= *Aes.* 276a); *Agamemnon* 717–736: "The Young Lion" (not in *Aes.*).

Sophocles (496–406), *Ajax* 1142–1149: "The Braggart" (not in *Aes.*); 1150–1158: "The Malicious Gloater" (not in *Aes.*).

Herodotus (ca. 485–425), *History* 1.141: "The Dancing Fish" (= *Aes.* 11a).

Aristophanes (ca. 445–386), *Wasps* 1401–1405: "Aesop and the Bitch" (= *Aes.* 423); 1427–1432: "The Sybarite Man" (= *Aes.* 428); 1435–1440: "The Sybarite Woman" (= *Aes.* 438); *Birds* 471–475: "The Crested Lark" (= *Aes.* 447).

Xenophon (ca. 430–355), *Memorabilia* 2.7.13–14: "The Sheep and the Dog" (= *Aes.* 356a).

Plato (427–347), *Phaedo* 60 B-C: "Pleasure and Pain" (= *Aes.* 445); *Phaedrus* 259 B-C: "The Cicadas" (= *Aes.* 470).

Aristotle (384–322), *Meteorologica* 356b11–17: "Aesop and the Ferryman" (~ *Aes.* 8); *Historia animalium* 619a17–20: "The Eagle" (= *Aes.* 422); *Politics* 1284a15–17: "The Lions and the Hares" (= *Aes.* 450); *Rhetoric* 1393b10–22: "The Stag, the Hare, and the Man" (= *Aes.* 269a); 1393b22–1394a1: "The Fox and the Hedgehog" (= *Aes.* 427).

2. References to Fables

Solon (ca. 640–560), frag. 11 West (→ *Aes.* 142). Theognis (mid-sixth century), 347–348 (→ *Aes.* 133); 602 (→ *Aes.* 176). Simonides (556–468), 9 = frag. 514 Page (→ *Aes.* 425). Timocreon (first half fifth century), 3 = frag. 729 Page (→ *Aes.* 17). Aeschylus, *Agamemnon* 355–361 (→ *Aes.* 282). Aristophanes, *Wasps* 1446–1448 and *Peace* 129–130 (→ *Aes.* 3); *Birds* 651–653 (→ *Aes.* 1). Plato, *Alcibiades* (1) 123 A (→ *Aes.* 142). Aristotle, *De partibus animalium* 663a35–663b3 (→ *Aes.* 100).

In the following cases it is not clear whether the author narrated the fable in full or merely alluded to it:

Ps.-Homer, *Margites* (seventh century) frag. 5 West (not in *Aes.*). Ibycus (mid-sixth century), 61 = frag. 342 Page (→ *Aes.* 458). Timocreon, 8 = frag. 734 Page (→ *Aes.* 425).

Given that the earliest surviving fable is found in Hesiod (*Works and Days* 202–212), the question as to possible pre-Greek origins for the genre itself can be expected from the first to produce a fairly reliable answer. Hesiod's short narrative—the hawk tells the nightingale wailing in his talons how pointless it is to struggle in the face of superior strength—appears within a didactic epic, where it is used as an exemplum in a passage discussing the relationship between power and justice. And ethics, illustrated on occasion with a fable, form the subject matter of one branch of Mesopotamian didactic literature on which, as is now widely believed by scholars, Hesiod very probably drew extensively: the ancient books of wisdom from Sumer and Akkad. These works—the oldest extant representative is *The Wisdom of Šuruppak,* written around 2500 B.C.—had an enormous influence on the literature of the various eastern Mediterranean cultures. One particularly important product of this tradition is the *Book of Ahikar,* the maxims of an Assyrian court official. The text, now pieced together from eleven fragments of fifth-century B.C. Aramaic papyri, even uses a motif also found in Hesiod's epic: the speaker presenting the moral teachings has suffered some kind of injustice.

None of the cuneiform Sumerian texts so far discovered actually contain a didactic exemplum that is directly related to the one in Hesiod. Nevertheless, the narrative works found on the clay tablets display such close thematic and formal similarities to Greco-Roman fable literature that Mesopotamia may safely be regarded as the original home of this genre. If we look at the second oldest of the texts listed above—the fable in Archilochus about the eagle who betrays his friend the fox and is punished by Zeus at the request of the latter (frag. 172–181 West)—we can very easily distinguish the way in which a source could be adapted. In this case the original text, the contents of which can be deduced from the beginning of the Akkadian *Etana* epic (ca. 1800 B.C.), showed the eagle confronted with its 'natural enemy,' the snake. Archilochus, in a verbal attack on his promise-breaking father-in-law, Lycambes, was using the fable situation to illustrate his own, and, since he identified himself with the fable character betrayed by a friend, it was only natural that he should wish his counterpart to have more pronounced retaliatory abilities. For the snake he therefore substituted the animal known for particular cunning, the fox (who probably also stood for him in the fable of the ape and the fox [frag. 185–187 West]).

Further exploration of such Near Eastern influences is not feasible within the bounds of this introduction, especially since literature on these Babylonian texts has long reached vaster proportions than available studies on the Greek fable. It only remains to note here that awareness of how deeply rooted the Greek fable was in the ancient Semitic world never completely faded among fable writers of classical antiquity. At the end of the second century A.D., or some time before this, Babrius wrote in the prologue to the second book of his *Fables in Iambics* that the fable was "an invention of the ancient Syrians who once lived under Ninus and Belus" (vv. 1–3). And the anonymous author of the second/third-century *Aesop Romance* based one lengthy section of his work (chapters 101–123) on the *Book of Ahikar*, thus equating the ancient Assyrian teacher of wisdom with the Greek λογοποιός (literally "storyteller") Aesop.

This is the term used as early as the mid-fifth century B.C. for the man under whose name fable books were still in circulation in late antiquity. According to Herodotus, the λογοποιός Aesop was a slave on the island of Samos at the beginning of the sixth century (2.134–135 = *Test.* 13 Perry). However, even the historian's early testimony bears traces of the Aesop legend that was to become more and more elaborate as it was told over the centuries in different contexts (we shall be returning to this later in connection with the book "The Life and Fables of Aesop"). One may therefore well doubt whether the λογοποιός ever actually existed in real life. But the Greeks certainly regarded him as the architect of the genre *fable*, and it was his authority that was popularly cited, even into Byzantine times, when a fable was to be told or alluded to in passing. This perception can be traced from the oldest surviving reference of the kind, verse 1401 in Aristophanes' *Wasps* (422 B.C.), through all periods of Greek literature. Moreover, it is not entirely implausible that there did once live in archaic times an especially talented fable teller named Aesop. It would, after all, be safe to say that the narrative texts brought from Mesopotamia only circulated in very rare cases as actual reading material, because the books of wisdom were written in a foreign language. It is much more reasonable to assume that, between the eighth and fifth centuries B.C., Greek familiarity with originally Babylonian fable literature was based almost exclusively on oral tradition. And who better to tell such fables than natives of the Near East now living in Greece, for example, educated citizens from the towns of Asia Minor who had been carried off as slaves? Perhaps in the end there really is some historical truth behind the legendary λογοποιός Aesop who lived in bondage on Samos.

On the other hand, the details of Aesop's origins vary: alongside testimonies describing him as a Thracian, there are later ones that have him hail from Phrygia or Lydia (*Test.* 4–7 Perry). This corresponds strikingly to the variety of labels which appear now and again, from the archaic period onward, as an alternative to "Aesopic" when ancient authors for some reason mention the origins of the fable: "Libyan," "Egyptian," "Carian," "Cyprian," "Lydian," "Phrygian," "Cilician," or "Sybarite" (Hausrath 1909, 1719–1723; *Test.* 85–93 Perry). The criteria for such classifications are vague, if not entirely obscure. On the other hand, seven of the adjectives do have one thing in common: the proper names from which they derive all stand for regions that once, before Alexander's conquests, belonged to the vast empires of Mesopotamia (including Assyria). And the Greeks used the word "Sybarite" proverbially as a synonym for "luxurious, effeminate" to describe a way of life which, according to popular preconceptions, was characteristic for the entire Eastern world. It could be, then, that the legend of Aesop somehow—in a way we can no longer trace—reflects the 'invasion' of Greece by the fables of the East, and that Aesop ought accordingly to be seen not as a historical figure, but rather as a sort of mythic embodiment of the typical Hellenized storyteller from the Semitic Orient.

What the figure of Aesop definitely does not personify is the common people's spirit of rebellion against oppressive rule, as was first maintained by O. Crusius in an article of 1913. This theory may have found, even quite recently so, considerable echo— Spoerri (1942–43), for example, coined the phrase "the Fable's Revolt"—but there is nothing in the thirty-two Greek fables we know of from the archaic and classical periods that corroborates it. A confrontation between the weak and the strong only appears twice in these texts: in "The Hawk and the Nightingale" in Hesiod (*Works and Days* 202–212), and in "The Eagle and the Dung Beetle" (*Aes.* 3), to which Aristophanes refers twice (*Wasps* 1446–1448; *Peace* 129–130), and which Semonides possibly inserted into one of his iambic poems (frag. 13 West). In Hesiod, whose version of the theme survives in full, the authority of the "kings" to whom the poet addresses his exemplary tale is never actually questioned: he just appeals to them not to found their actions simply on the rights of the more powerful, as the hawk did. One of the main reasons for this erroneous assumption that the early Greek fables voice social criticism was probably a theory put forward by Phaedrus on the rise of the genre (3. *prol.* 33–37; see below, p. 48).

In point of fact, one characteristic of the above-listed verse and prose fables from the eighth to the fourth centuries B.C. is not any noticeable concentration on one specific ideological message, but instead the very plurality of their perspectives. When, for example, a fable is employed in the way recommended by Aristotle (see above, p. 11) as a rhetorical argument, then it can just as easily also serve, within the context of a political discussion, to clarify the standpoint of someone in a position of power. We find one such instance from the period which interests us at the moment in Herodotus 1.141: there King Cyrus of Persia tells the fable of the dancing fish in order to illustrate the situation of the Ionian cities he is currently threatening. And from a later period in the genre's history we have another example: the fable of the limbs' revolt against the belly, which, in Livy 2.32.5–12, Menenius Agrippa uses to persuade the plebeians to end their 'strike.' The diversity of themes which we find in the fables used for rhetorical purposes in extant Greek and Roman texts cannot be discussed in any depth here, but we do at least have room to name the relevant passages:

Sophocles, *Ajax* 1142–1158 (not in *Aes.*). Herodotus, 1.141 (= *Aes.* 11a). Aristotle, *Rhetoric* 1393b10–1394a1 (= *Aes.* 269a and 427). Pompeius Trogus (late first century A.D.), *Historiae Philippicae* in Justinus's epitome 43.4.4 (~ *Aes.* 480). Livy (59 B.C.–A.D. 17), *Ab urbe condita* 2.32.5–12 (~ *Aes.* 130; cf. also Dionysius of Halicarnassus, *Antiquitates Romanae* 6.83.2, 86.3, and Plutarch [see below], *Coriolanus* 6.3). Diodorus (first century B.C.), *Bibliotheca* 19.25.5–6 (~ *Aes.* 140); 33.7.5–6 (~ *Aes.* 31). Flavius Josephus (A.D. 37–ca. 95), *Antiquitates Iudaicae* 18.5.174–175 (~ *Aes.* 427). Plutarch (ca. A.D. 46–120), *Themistocles* 18.6 (= *Aes.* 441); *Phocion* 9.2 (~ *Aes.* 245); *Demosthenes* 23.4–6 (~ *Aes.* 153); *Moralia* 112A-B (= *Aes.* 462), 848 A-B (= *Aes.* 460; cf. also *Aes.* 63). Appianus (second century A.D.), *Bella Civilia* 1.101 (= *Aes.* 471).

Hesiod's fable, already mentioned here and for us the starting point in the genre's history, is also at the forefront insofar as it is the first of those fables which are used in ancient literature for philosophical reasoning. To these belong, from the classical period of Greek literature, the texts listed above (pp. 12–13) under Xenophon, Plato, and Aristotle; distantly related too are the passages (p. 13) from the poems of the elegists Solon and Theognis and the lyric poets Ibycus, Simonides, and Timocreon, as well as those from the plays of the tragedian Aeschylus. Fables inserted as exempla for philosophical ideas also appear in authors from the imperial age, for instance, Horace, Plutarch, Lucian, and Maximus of Tyre—in authors, then, who each represent different systems of thought. Clearly, appreciation and exploitation of the fable's exemplifying qualities were not restricted to any one school. As the passages in Xenophon and Plato would seem to show, Socrates liked to illustrate his teachings with the kind of simple, straightforward example the fable provided. We are told that, while in prison awaiting execution, he rendered Aesopica into verse (Plato, *Phaedrus* 60D–61B = *Test.* 73 Perry), and we may conclude from this that he felt particularly drawn to Aesop, who, according to legend, was likewise sentenced to death for impiety.

Alongside their appearance in philosophical discussions, fables can also be found from earliest times onward within Greek poetic genres where the authors are in some way offering 'truth with a smile,' in texts, then, which modern reading would classify as satirical in tone. Such use begins, as the above survey shows (pp. 12–13), with the comic epic ascribed to Homer, *Margites*, the iambic poems of Archilochus and Semonides, and the comedies of Aristophanes; it is continued in the iambic poetry of Callimachus (ca. 300–240 B.C.), and in the second/first century B.C. it reaches Roman literature, where we find fables in the satires of Ennius, Lucilius, and Horace. The function with which, in varying degrees, all of these authors invest the fable—that of serving as illustration to help expose human follies and vices—had an unmistakable influence on fable-book authors who intended their work as literature in its own right, principally on Phaedrus and the author of the *Collectio Augustana*, but certainly also on Babrius, Avianus, and the anonymous who wrote the *Aesopus Latinus*. And three Greek literary texts, which were very probably based in essence on fable motifs—Aristophanes' *Peace* (→ *Aes.* 3), the mock-heroic epic *Batrachomyomachia* (→ *Aes.* 384), and the *Ass Romance*, perhaps written by Lucian, of which only the epitome (Ps.-Lucian) *Lucius, or The Ass* survives (→ *Aes.* 91, 164, 179, 182)—can also be classified in the very broadest of senses as satire.

We have now seen that the fable lent itself to illustrative use within a variety of prose and verse genres found in ancient literature, and it ought to be clear that attempts to determine any uniform tenor or desired effect common to all the texts face serious difficulties. Nevertheless, scholars have naturally always tried to formulate some kind of definition for the genre. Indeed, as one might expect, the subject occupies much space in literature on the fable. Those basing their approach on modern fable theories meet, however, with considerable problems when applying their concepts to antiquity's Aesopica. Let us look, for example, at the question of subgenres. Even in the archaic period a fable could consist not only of the short narrative form that defines it today—a text culminating in a moral expressed by one of the two characters involved (see below)—it could also be an explanatory legend (*aition:* cf. above Ibycus, 61 = frag. 342 Page; Aristophanes, *Birds* 471–475; Plato, *Phaedo* 60 B-C, *Phaedrus* 259 B-C; and Aristotle, *Historia animalium* 619a17–20) or a 'vying match' between two rivals. For this latter type, which is also found in Eastern wisdom literature, there are no extant archaic or classical Greek examples, but it is used as a fable motif by Callimachus. In the fourth of his *Iambi* (frag. 194 Pfeiffer), the laurel tree vies with the olive tree, in imitation, the poet says, of a "Lydian" model (vv. 6–8). This form as such, then, probably also made its way into Greek literature before the third century B.C.

Or we could take the fable's cast. Here too the ancient texts display, by the modern standards which equate *fable* with *animal fable*, a great deal of variability. In the above-listed thirty-two fables from early times, the tales involving animals alone represent the largest group, and this also applies to the ancient fables of later periods. However, relatively often we also find here fables which feature a human and an animal (e.g., Aeschylus, *Agamemnon* 717–736 or Aristophanes, *Wasps* 1401–1405, where Aesop himself appears). Further, the cast can consist of a human and an inanimate object (Aristophanes, *Wasps* 1435–1440), humans only (Sophocles, *Ajax* 1142–1158; Aristophanes, *Wasps* 1427–1432; Aristotle, *Meteorologica* 356b11–17 [with Aesop appearing again]), gods and animals (Plato, *Phaedrus* 259 B-C; Aristophanes, *Wasps* 1446–1448 and *Peace* 129–130 [→ Aes. 3]), gods only (Aristotle, *De partibus animalium* 663a35–663b3 [→ Aes. 100]), or personifications (Plato, *Phaedo* 60 B-C). There have been many attempts to find a definition of the genre that takes cognizance of this diversity, but the most convincing one is still the description found in the rhetors Theon (first/second century A.D.) and Aphthonius (fourth/fifth century A.D.): μῦθός ἐστι λόγος ψευδὴς εἰκονίζων ἀλήθειαν (*Test.* 102–103 Perry: "a fable is a fictional narrative which portrays a truth," i.e., from which can be gathered a truth applicable in real life [a moral]).

Given the fable's broad spectrum of contents, it is somewhat surprising that the outward form of Aesopica already presents a relatively uniform picture in archaic and classical times. This, of course, makes it all the easier for us to regard the texts, themselves termed varyingly αἶνος, μῦθος and λόγος by their authors— all three words can mean "story"—as members of the same group. The oldest Greek fables even display something like formulaic phraseology of the kind later to be used systematically by the author of the *Collectio Augustana*. This is very evident at those points where the narrator, after finishing a fable inserted into the text, explains to the audience or readers the conclusion they are expected to draw from the exemplum: "Thus you too . . ." (οὕτω δὲ καὶ ὑμεῖς/σύ . . . : Sophocles, *Ajax* 1147; Aristophanes, *Wasps* 1432; Aristotle, *Rhetoric* 1393b18–19), or a similar expression (cf. Aeschylus, *Agamemnon* 739; Sophocles, *Ajax* 1158; Xenophon, *Memorabilia* 7.14; Aristotle, *Rhetoric* 1393b31).

Leaving aside the etiological fables, we find that, of the fifteen narratives which survive in their entirety—all except one of these (Aeschylus, *Myrmidones* frag. 139 Radt) involve two characters— nine actually end with a remark that comments on the events recounted. The words are spoken by one of the figures, and the moral exemplified by the story can be derived from what is said; in several cases the closing comment censures the other character's behavior. The preceding events are sometimes divided into an exposition and the action proper, so that the fable as a whole is then tripartite. This is actually seldom the case in the surviving texts from archaic and classical periods, but later fables are frequently structured in this way. Alternatively, the fable can simply be made up of two parts: action and closing remark.

One example of a tripartite fable can be found in Aristophanes, *Wasps* 1435–1440, a text in which this pattern is clearly already being parodied:

Ἐν Συβάρει γυνή ποτε
κατέαξ᾽ ἐχῖνον.
[listener's comment]
Οὐχῖνος οὖν ἔχων τιν᾽ ἐπεμαρτύρατο·
εἶθ᾽ ἡ Συβαρῖτις εἶπεν· Εἰ ναὶ τὰν Κόραν
τὴν μαρτυρίαν ταύτην ἐάσας ἐν τάχει
ἐπίδεσμον ἐπρίω, νοῦν ἂν εἶχες πλείονα.᾽

[1] In Sybaris a woman *once* broke a jar. [2] *So* the jar called someone to bear witness to this. [3] *Then* the Sybarite woman said: "If, by Demeter, you had quickly gotten yourself a bandage instead of a witness, you would have been showing more sense."

The two-part fable can be seen in particularly simple form in the *scolion* ("drinking-song") written by an anonymous poet at the turn of the sixth to the fifth century B.C. (*Scolion* 9 = frag. 892 Page). This example ends, moreover, with the kind of gnomic remark found just three times in the early texts (cf. also Hesiod, *Works and Days* 210–211; Aristophanes, *Wasps* 1431):

Ὁ δὲ καρκίνος ὦδ᾽ ἔφα
χαλᾶι τὸν ὄφιν λαβών·
ἐὐθὺν χρὴ τὸν ἑταῖρον ἔμ-
μεν καὶ μὴ σκολιὰ φρονεῖν.᾽

The crab, having seized the snake with its pincers, now spoke thus: "A friend should be straight and not have crooked thoughts."

Only once in the early texts do we find a development which occurs frequently in the later fables, especially in the *Collectio Augustana:* the closing comment is spoken by a character who does not appear until near the end of the story. In Aristophanes' *Wasps* (1427–1432) a man from Sybaris falls off a chariot and hurts his head because he knows nothing about driving; a witness to the accident advises him that one should only turn one's hand to the skill one possesses.

Simple as these formal devices in the early Greek fables may be, our ability to recognize them as such will be extremely important when we come to a formal and stylistic evaluation of the texts written for fable books, of fables, that is, which were intended by their authors as literary pieces. Such fabulists would refine these narrative techniques.

THE HELLENISTIC FABLE *REPERTORIUM*

Two brief remarks made by Diogenes Laertius in his *Vitae philoso-phorum* tell us that the statesman and philosopher Demetrius of Phalerum (ca. 350–280 B.C.) published Aesopic fables in a book-roll (5.81: Αἰσωπείων α᾽), and that this represented a "collection" of Aesopica (5.80: λόγων Αἰσωπείων συναγωγαί). Since this is the old-est fable book on record, much thought has naturally been given to its possible contents and purpose, perhaps—as inevitably hap-pens when classicists are dealing with lost texts—a touch too much. Perry devotes an article of sixty pages to the matter (1962), Adrados, a chapter almost ninety pages long in his book on the *fábula greco-latina* (1979, 421–508). And yet we still cannot even be sure how to interpret the term *collection* here. Did Demetrius sim-ply assemble fables that were already circulating in written form? Or did he tell fables himself, either re-writing tales com-posed by other authors, or writing down fable material from oral traditions, or inventing new Aesopica?

There are good reasons for assuming that no fable books existed prior to Demetrius's λόγων Αἰσωπείων συναγωγαί. First, it is highly unlikely that books containing narrative prose texts would have been written during Greece's classical epoch, or indeed in archaic times, because fiction belonged to the realm of poetry. If λόγοι were 'narrated' in prose, then as episodes in historiographical works, but not as novellas or fables, and when the latter were not being used to illustrate a particular point, they were reserved exclusively for oral presentation. Second, *collecting* is an intellec-tual pursuit particularly characteristic of the Hellenistic age. This could find its outlet in the critical editing of older literature—that is, of early Greek lyric poetry—but also in the composition of ele-giac *Kollektivgedichte*, such as Callimachus's *Aetia*. Again, we do not know whether Demetrius's "collecting" of Aesopic fables was of a scholarly or of a creative nature. We are told, however, that he also gathered sayings of the "Seven Sages" and *chriae* for publica-tion, which may be taken as 'circumstantial evidence' that he fathered the idea of compiling the first Greek fable book.

As to the purpose of the λόγων Αἰσωπείων συναγωγαί, a look at Demetrius of Phalerum's other works and at his intellectual habitat again permits certain deductions. He was a pupil of the man who wrote what is now the oldest extant theoretical discussion of the genre: Aristotle. In his *Rhetoric* the philosopher, as we saw above (p. 11), had included the fable amongst the types of exempla suitable for use in rhetorical argumentation. Demetrius also tried his hand at this discipline—the list of his writings includes a *Rhetoric*—and it therefore seems likely that he decided to compile a practical *repertorium* to complement his teacher's guidelines for argumentation. Its contents may have been limited to fables on the grounds that Aristotle declared this type of example to be "suitable for popular oratory" (δημηγορικός). And such a book would not only have been read by rhetors, poets, and authors looking for suitable illustrations, but also by anyone seeking entertainment and moral instruction in one.

The theory—based on Perry's studies—that Demetrius's fable book was probably a sort of *promptuarium* referred to for all conceivable literary contexts, is borne out by the existence of one fragment in particular: *Papyrus Rylands 493,* in which fables are presented just as one would expect to find them in a handbook of this kind. The papyrus, dating from the first half of the first century A.D. and edited by C. H. Roberts in 1938, represents the remains of a fable book; it contains 157 lines in all, and, although many of these are half-mutilated, the surviving textual material is extremely valuable. In addition to the opening section of "The Horse and the Man" (lines 19–34 ~ *Aes.* 269), the papyrus offers almost complete versions of "The Shepherd and the Sheep" (lines 35–59 ~ *Aes.* 208), "Heracles and Plutus" (lines 75–ca. 97 ~ *Aes.* 111), and "The Owl and the Birds" (lines 101–131 ~ *Aes.* 437), as well as two opening and two closing sections of unidentifiable fables (lines 55–56, 72–74, 132, and 153–154). Moreover, a comparison of all the fable beginnings and endings in the papyrus—of the four just named, that is, together with lines 19–21, 35–37, 75–76, and 129–131 from the partially readable texts—interestingly proves that the unknown editor of this collection frames the exempla with stereotypical phrases.

In our discussion of the fables found in archaic and classical Greek literature, we observed that, when it comes to the moral of the tale, the proposed lesson is frequently introduced with a formulaic expression. The *Rylands* papyrus obviously cannot offer any direct parallels to such usage because its fables are not woven into a specific context; they stand instead one after the other, like poems in an anthology. Nevertheless, these texts too indicate what the intended *fabula docet* is, introducing their pointers immediately before the story proper with one of the said stereotypical phrases used to frame the fables: "[For a certain type of person] the following fable is applicable" (. . . ὅδε λόγος ἐφαρμόζει). And, correspondingly, the words spoken at the end of the fable proper by one of the characters—who thus, as we observed above, implicitly voices the *fabula docet*—are preceded by another stereotypical framing phrase: "he seems to have articulated the moral/maxim, saying . . ." (τὴν γνώμην φαίνεται εἰρηκέναι λέγων . . .). There follows the corresponding gnomic remark (these fables belong, then, to the type that closes with a γνώμη: see above, p. 21). Here is an example, indeed the only instance in the *Rylands* papyrus where a complete sentence is still legible after such a stereotypical phrase: "Thus all who commit an offence blame the gods" (οὕτως ἁμαρτάνων ἕκαστος αἰτιᾶται θεούς).

What was, then, the procedure when fables were collected for such a *promptuarium*? It began with their extraction from the context in which they had served as exemplum. We know from Aristotle's theoretical discussion how the first of the identifiable λόγοι in the *Rylands* papyrus—"The Horse and the Man"—was once applied to a given situation (*Rhetoric* 1393b10–22 = *Aes.* 269a). A fable's uncoupling did not mean, however, that it was disassociated from its didactic function. Each text was furnished with a 'caption' indicating which moral message the story could serve to exemplify. In the *Rylands* papyrus these captions—the technical term is *promythium*—were given some prominence by the scribe, who positioned the first letter of each so that it jutted out of the text block.

This form of presentation was, of course, extremely practical for rhetors, poets, and prose writers in search of a fable. They would find here not only the required material, but also a sort of 'subject index.' The *repertorium* would suit the needs of all users, as the style of the fables in the papyrus was the simplest conceivable, and the narration was confined essentially to a summary of the contents. Those looking for a λόγος to fit a particular theme would require nothing further, and the more concise the argumentum, the freer the authors or rhetors would be when adapting a story in form and content to their own subject. The Greek authors of imperial times who used fables as exempla—we shall be looking at them in the next chapter—include one who, in his speeches on popular morality, twice retold one fable found in the *Rylands* papyrus ("The Owl and the Birds"), each time in a very different way: Dio of Prusa (*Orations* 12.7–8 = *Aes.* 437, and *Orations* 72.13–16 = *Aes.* 437a).

Before we turn our attention to Dio and his contemporaries, let us sum up our findings so far. The history of ancient fable books begins with the Hellenistic fable *repertorium,* the compilers of which laid no claims to their literary quality, but simply aimed to provide rhetors and writers with a convenient source of useful material. It seems probable that this type of collection was 'invented' by Demetrius of Phalerum; we have some idea of what his λόγων Αἰσωπείων συναγωγαί may have looked like from our knowledge of a fable-book fragment—*Papyrus Rylands 493*—dating from the first half of the first century A.D. A text of this kind would have served not only as *promptuarium* for reference purposes, but also possibly—as we shall see shortly—as a source for fable books written in imperial times, although this is an assumption that borders closely on mere speculation. And were we to debate whether the tangible fable-book remains in the *Rylands* papyrus in fact represent, as Perry believes, what is left of Demetrius's collection, we would most definitely be speculating. Such musings would in any case mean devoting undue attention to a text that has been lost—one of the very grooves in which this introduction to the ancient fable was planning not to travel.

THE IMPERIAL AGE

In Greek literature of the period to which we now turn—the first to the fourth centuries A.D.—fables other than those collected in books are again employed as exempla in varying contexts and also (probably in continuation of a earlier tradition we can no longer trace) as the subject of exercises in rhetoric schools. Almost all authors who used fables for the purpose of exemplification belonged to the Greek intellectual and cultural elite of a period known as the Second Sophistic. A thorough knowledge of rhetoric was seen as prerequisite for every form of elite education, with the result that rhetors, whether teachers or itinerant professional speakers, played a leading role in Greek cultural life under the Roman Empire.

Furthermore, rhetorical devices became a characteristic feature of every kind of literary writing, from the philosophical and scientific treatise to the fictional narrative. All of these could be given the outward appearance of an oration or form part of one.

From six authors of such lectures and orations there survive texts in which fables are used: Dio of Prusa (ca. 40–120), Maximus of Tyre (ca. 125–185), Aelius Aristides (129–ca.189), Himerius (ca. 310–380), Libanius (314–ca. 393), and Themistius (ca. 317–388). As far as the history of the fable is concerned, the most interesting of these is Dio of Prusa, who in a sense identifies with Aesop. In *Orations* 72, where he talks of his role as philosopher-darling of his audiences (he lived for some years as a wandering preacher of Stoic-Cynic thought), he names Socrates, Diogenes, the "Seven Sages," Aesop, and himself in one breath. He also stresses, however, that he and the other philosophers of his day cannot compare to the great teachers of wisdom. At this point he tells the "Aesopic" fable of the owl, which the other birds learn to admire for its sagacity (*Orations* 72.13–16; cf. Dio's other version of this fable in *Orations* 12.7–8).

We find a parallel to this association of Aesop with the "Seven Sages" not only in the fictional biography of the fabulist, which may have been published in Dio's lifetime, but also in a work of Plutarch's, who was roughly contemporary with Dio. In his *Dinner of the Seven Sages* Plutarch has Aesop take part, and seats him on a stool at the feet of Solon, Athenian statesman and one of the seven (ca. 640–560 B.C.). Plutarch seems to have been very interested in Aesop and Aesopic fables, as we may conclude not only from the dinner scene, but perhaps also from his lost but listed μύθων βιβλία γ' ("three books of fables"?), and definitely from his use of fables in several works that have survived. In the *Moralia*—treatises and dialogues mostly on questions of popular philosophy—the last count registered twenty-three passages in which the author either narrates, paraphrases, or alludes to fables, and in the *Lives* a further eight (supra, p. 17). Of these fables a total of eleven (= *Aes.* 433, 434, 440, 441, 446, 449, 453, 460,

462, 467, 468) are actually only known to us through Plutarch, which suggests either that he had read them in a fable book that has not survived, or that he composed them himself, using the "Aesopic" pattern.

Exactly how fables were handled by Greek-speaking authors of the imperial age can only be properly explored in some future study devoted to just that. We must content ourselves for the moment with a closer look at the most important and ultimately most influential of these writers: Lucian of Samosata (ca. 120–180). A great many of the references to fables found in his works noticeably consist of brief allusions, and so the reader is clearly expected to possess a certain prior knowledge of Greek fable literature. An example: the hero of the dialogue *Icaromenippus* says that he had founded his hopes of flying up to the heavens on, amongst other things, "Aesop's" tales of "eagles and beetles, even camels" who had managed the trip (chap. 10). Not even every ancient reader would have known that this alludes to "The Eagle and the Dung Beetle" (*Aes.* 3) and "The Camel and Zeus" (*Aes.* 117). Perhaps we may therefore conclude from this type of 'quotation' that Lucian and his audience were already familiar with the now-lost "Life and Fables of Aesop," which we can only reconstruct on the basis of the *Aesop Romance* and the *Collectio Augustana,* and which, as we shall see later, could have been circulating in the mid-second century (infra, p. 75). Neither Lucian nor any of the other authors of the imperial age who use fables as exempla mention this book; if they cite a source at all, then they cite "Aesop," but this could simply stand for oral tradition or a fable *repertorium.* And yet there is one characteristic that Lucian's writings, the *Aesop Romance,* and the *Collectio Augustana* all have in common: a fondness for witty satire and caustic ridicule.

This shared penchant finds expression in, for example, the frequency with which all three expose the discrepancy between appearance and reality. In the fables retold or called briefly to the well-versed reader's mind by Lucian, this motif occurs four times:

1. In his longest version of the fable where Momus, who is fault-finding personified, criticizes the creations of three gods (*Aes.* 100), Lucian confines himself to relating one alleged failing of

Hephaestus's work: man, as there is no window in the human breast through which to look into the soul (*Hermotimus* 20; cf. *Nigrinus* 32, and *True Story* 2.3).

2. Lucian twice mentions the fable of the ass which dons a lion's skin and goes around scaring people (*The Fisherman* 32; *The Runaways* 13 = *Aes*. 188).

3. In *Pseudologistes* (chap. 5) Lucian alludes to the jackdaw which dresses itself in borrowed plumes (*Aes*. 101).

4. The fable "The Dancing Apes" in *The Fisherman* (chap. 36) is told in particularly witty fashion; it was possibly Lucian's own invention (based on *Aes*. 50 and 107?), as it is the earliest extant version of the story (*Aes*. 463; cf. Gregory of Nyssa, *De professione Christiana* pp. 131–133 Jaeger). In illustration of the use of fables as exempla in imperial times, let us pause here to read Lucian's story.

Λέγεται δὲ καὶ βασιλεύς τις Αἰγύπτιος πιθήκους ποτὲ πυρριχίζειν διδάξαι καὶ τὰ θηρία - μιμηλότατα δέ ἐστι τῶν ἀνθρωπίνων - ἐκμαθεῖν τάχιστα καὶ ὀρχεῖσθαι ἀλουργίδας ἀμπεχόμενα καὶ προσωπεῖα περικείμενα, καὶ μέχρι γε πολλοῦ εὐδοκιμεῖν τὴν θέαν, ἄχρι δὴ θεατής τις ἀστεῖος κάρυα ὑπὸ κόλπον ἔχων ἀφῆκεν εἰς τὸ μέσον· οἱ δὲ πίθηκοι ἰδόντες καὶ ἐκλαθόμενοι τῆς ὀρχήσεως, τοῦθ' ὅπερ ἦσαν, πίθηκοι ἐγένοντο ἀντὶ πυρριχιστῶν καὶ συνέτριβον τὰ προσωπεῖα καὶ τὴν ἐσθῆτα κατερρήγνυον καὶ ἐμάχοντο περὶ τῆς ὀπώρας πρὸς ἀλλήλους, τὸ δὲ σύνταγμα τῆς πυρρίχης διελέλυτο καὶ κατεγελᾶτο ὑπὸ τοῦ θεάτρου.

It is said, too, that a king of Egypt once taught apes to dance, and that the animals, as they are very apt at imitating human ways, learned quickly and gave an exhibition, with purple mantles about them and masks on their faces. For a long time the show, they say, went well, until a facetious spectator, having nuts in his pocket, tossed them into the midst. On catching sight of them, the monkeys forgot their dance, changed from artists of the ballet to the simians that they really were, smashed their masks, tore their costumes, and fought with each other for the nuts; whereby the carefully planned ballet was entirely broken up, and was laughed at by the spectators.

Uncovering the incongruity of appearance and reality is likely to have been one significant element in the lost *Metamorphoses of Lucius of Patrai*, the source for Apuleius's *Golden Ass*. Lucian may

possibly have been the author of this Greek novel, and it is therefore worth noting here that an epitome of the book—transmitted
amongst Lucian's writings under the title *Lucius, or The Ass*—features several motifs clearly derived from fables (cf. the survey in
H. van Thiel, *Der Eselsroman* [Munich 1971], 1:184–186). And a
number of those fables are also found in the *Collectio Augustana,*
one of them indeed—"The Ass and the Gardener"—(*Aes.* 179)
only there.

Concluding this discussion of the fables introduced as exempla in Greek literature, we turn now briefly to the teaching
method involved when imperial Greece's budding speakers and
writers were being shown how to use fables as a means of argumentation.

In Aristophanes' *Birds* a character is scolded with the words
"You are uneducated and not of an inquiring mind and you
haven't thumbed your Aesop" (v. 471: ἀμαθὴς γὰρ ἔφυς κοὐ
πολυπράγμων, οὐδ᾽ Αἴσωπον πεπάτηκας). This would seem to indicate that, in the fifth century B.C., fables already constituted in
some form part of the elementary curriculum. The earliest surviving schoolbooks which offer us some idea of such lessons only
date, however, from the first to the fifth centuries A.D. Their
authors are the rhetoricians Theon of Alexandria (first/second
century), Hermogenes (ca. 160–225), Aphthonius (fourth/fifth
century), and Nicolaus of Myra (born ca. A.D. 430). In addition, a
brief remark in the *Institutio oratoria* ("Education in Oratory") of
Quintilian (ca. 35–100) shows that a similar course of study was
required of students in imperial Rome (1.9.2 = *Test.* 97 Perry). We
also have fable texts written on wax tablets by third-century students in Palmyra (*Tabulae Assendelftianae,* Leiden) and, likewise,
on papyrus fragments from the first/second to the fifth centuries
(*PMichigan 457; POxy. 1404; PAmherst II.26; PGrenfell II.84*).

Working with fables formed part of the rhetoric student's
preparatory studies, that is, of the *progymnasmata;* these exercises
are described in textbooks bearing this name by the four above-
listed authors (cf. the relevant passages in Perry 1952, *Test.* 101–104).
Fables were, then, the first literary writings with which students
had to acquaint themselves. They cropped up initially as dictation
pieces—this is documented by the wax tablets from Palmyra—
and as texts to be learnt by rote and rendered in other words;

POxy. 1404 (third century A.D.) has preserved an impression of such assignments' possible results, in this case a somewhat clumsy Latin précis of "The Dog Carrying Meat" (*Aes.* 133). At the beginning of the *praeexercitamenta,* fables were then the subject of grammatical and metrical studies; the version of "The Murderer" (*Aes.* 32) found in *PGrenfell II.84* clearly represents a fifth/sixth-century Egyptian student's attempt to recast a verse fable into prose. Finally, translating was practiced on fable texts; samples of this can be seen in Ps.-Dositheus's *Hermeneumata,* which we shall be looking at more closely below, and also in the bilingual *PAmherst II.26* (third/fourth century), with its poor Latin version of Babrius 16 and 17. Moreover, a general idea of how one more mature student set about learning Greek can be gained from the unfortunately very fragmentary text of "The Swallow and the Birds" (*Aes.* 39) in *PMichigan 457* (first/second century).

At a more advanced level within the highly organized system of *progymnasmata,* style, content, and possible applications of fables became the focus of attention. A text would either be fleshed out with an elaborate characterization of the figures involved and more background detail, or it would be reduced to the core of its message. The ultimate goal of all these exercises—the ability to introduce a fable with maximum effect into a speech in order to illustrate a point—was then reached by way of assignments involving the *fabula docet.* Students had to think of a historical event to which the moral of the tale could be applied, or they had to reinterpret the fable, reaching a moral conclusion different from the one traditionally attached to it. Or—and this was doubtlessly the final, most difficult exercise—they would be given a maxim for which they had to invent their own original fable.

Babrius's *Fables in Iambics* appears to have been an especially popular choice of text for these rhetorical *progymnasmata.* Of the fourteen fables we find on the Palmyra wax tablets, eleven are from this book. In the *Hermeneumata,* a schoolbook erroneously handed down under the name of Dositheus (fourth century A.D.) and actually from the early third century A.D., nine of the sixteen fables featured were very probably based on Babrius (1–3, 6, 7, 9, 11, 14, 16), and another three most likely on now-lost *mythiambi* (10, 12, 15). The fables in Ps.-Dositheus—a 'Latin Primer' for Greeks—form the fourth of twelve central chapters in which students were offered first a Greek-Latin vocabulary and then a series of short, simple texts in both languages, these intended as exercises. In contrast to modern bilingual books, where continuous texts in each language appear parallel to one another, the Greek and Latin are presented piecemeal, with a word or phrase in the former always followed immediately by its equivalent in the latter. Thus the beginning of the famous fable "The Fox and the Crow" (*Aes.* 124), for example, reads: Κοραξ· τυρον· αρπασας *Coruus· caseum· rapuit* | και· επανω· δενδρου· *etsuper arborem* | πετασθις· εκαθισεν *uolans sedit* (Goetz [1892] 43 = Ps.-Dositheus 9).

The fables in the *Hermeneumata* are rendered in a very simple style to suit the needs of students learning a new language. It is therefore unlikely that the book's anonymous author hoped to have the little collection numbered amongst the fable books written with a view to literary fame. The rhetor Aphthonius was no doubt similarly unambitious when writing his forty fables; these were probably published simply as a supplement to his *Progymnasmata.* Here too Babrius was the source for many of the texts: for twenty-four almost certainly (3, 5, 9, 11, 13, 16, 25, 29, 36, 43, 44, 72, 77, 79, 93, 103, 108, 109, 120, 122, 137, 139, 140, frag. 21 Luzz.), and for others conceivably so. Aphthonius presents texts which constitute little more than a brief abstract (cf., for example, no. 26 and Babrius 108) alongside other fables retold in a quite animated style (e.g., no. 29; cf. Babrius 77), but such a mixture is entirely in keeping with the *Progymnasmata*'s mixture of instructions for condensing and elaborating on fables. For the moment the forty μῦθοι here may therefore be added to the list of Greek fable texts which owe their existence primarily to a literary and rhetorical device, that of illustrating a point with a narrative. However, closer examination of these hitherto rather neglected texts might one day reveal a different picture.

■ Roman Literature

The fable of the limbs rebelling against the belly, which Livy has Menenius Agrippa tell to the insurgent plebeians, is introduced by the historian with the following words: "he is said to have told this . . . in the antiquated and primitive style of the times" (2.32.8: *prisco illo dicendi et horrido modo . . . hoc narrasse fertur*). As

P. L. Schmidt (1979) rightly observed, Livy, writing in the classical period of Roman literature, is indicating here his disapproval of a rhetorical convention that allows political arguments to be illustrated not by way of *exempla maiorum*, but with a facile fable. In a similar vein, Quintilian declares in his *Institutio oratoria* that fables tended to sway primarily the rural population and the uneducated, these being credulous audiences that liked a good story and would readily agree to anything that has afforded them pleasure (5.11.19 = *Test.* 98 Perry: *fabellae . . . ducere animos solent praecipue rusticorum et imperitorum qui et simplicius quae ficta sunt audiunt, et capti voluptate facile iis, quibus delectantur, consentiunt*).

Little wonder, then, that the passages in which Roman poets or prose writers illustrate their thoughts with a fable, or a reference to such, can be listed in two shakes of a lamb's tail.

Ennius (239–169 B.C.), *Satires* frag. 21–58 Vahlen: "The Crested Lark" (~ *Aes.* 325).

Lucilius (died ca. 102 B.C.), *Satires* frag. 1074–1081 Krenkel: "The Lion and the Fox" (~ *Aes.* 142).

Catullus (ca. 87–54 B.C.), *Carmina* 22.21 (→ *Aes.* 266).

Horace (65–8 B.C.), *Satires* 2.1.64 (→ *Aes.* 188); 3.186 (→ *Aes.* 394?); 3.299 (→ *Aes.* 266); 3.314–320: "The Frog and the Calf" (~ *Aes.* 376); 5.55–56 (→ *Aes.* 124); 6.79–117: "Town Mouse and Country Mouse" (~ *Aes.* 352); *Odes* 1.16.13–16 (→ *Aes.* 240); *Epistles* 1.1.73–75 (→ *Aes.* 142); 3.18–20 (→ *Aes.* 101); 7.29–33: "The Fox with a Swollen Belly" (~ *Aes.* 24); 10.34–41: "The Horse and the Man" (~ *Aes.* 269a); 20.14–16 (→ *Aes.* 186).

Pompeius Trogus (late first century B.C.), *Historiae Philippicae*, in Justinus's epitome 43.4.4: "The Dog and Her Puppies" (~ *Aes.* 480).

Livy (59 B.C.–A.D. 17), *Ab urbe condita* 2.32.5–12: "The Belly and the Limbs" (~*Aes.* 130).

Seneca (ca. 4–65), *De otio* 1.3 (→ *Aes.* 142).

Martial (ca. 40–102), *Epigrams* 10.79.9–10 (→ Aes. 376).

Fronto (ca. 100–170), *Epistles* p. 152 van den Hout: "The Vine and the Holly Oak" (not in *Aes.*).

Apuleius (born ca. 125), *Praefatio* to *De Deo Socratis* 4.108–111: "The Crow and the Fox" (~ *Aes.* 124).

Gellius (born ca. 130), *Noctes Atticae* 2.29.3–16: "The Crested
   Lark" (~ *Aes.* 325).

Among these fables, it must be noted, many appear within a
genre thought to have been 'invented' in Rome: verse satire. Long
before Horace wrote his version of "Town Mouse and Country
Mouse"—one of the most famous fable texts of antiquity—
Ennius created his tale of the crested lark, two verses of which
we find still quoted in the second century A.D. by Aulius Gellius.
The lines represent the moral attached to the fable proper and
betray the poet's familiarity with the Greek "Thus you too . . ."
formula (supra, p. 20):

> *Hoc erit tibi argumentum semper in promptum situm:*
> *Ne quid exspectes amicos quod tute agere possies.*

This is the lesson you should always keep in mind: that you should not
expect of friends anything that you can do yourself.

Ennius's rendering of the crested lark fable—now lost apart from
these two closing verses—is only mentioned by Gellius after he
has presented his own version of the *apologus* and then stressed
that one can learn as much from this as from philosophical discussions on the theme. We have absolutely no reason to suppose
that Gellius is simply paraphrasing Ennius's text and even borrowing certain expressions, and yet editors and translators of the
latter's *Saturae*, together with scholars compiling anthologies of
fables, would have us believe that Gellius's version is in fact a
fragment of Ennius; they therefore unfailingly reproduce it immediately before the two extant verses. Historicistic logic again: if
there was a source, there must be a faithful copy.

  It was probably Lucilius who first used verse satire for attacks
on personal enemies and thus linked the genre, among other
things, to the Greek iambic tradition. It would have been interesting to see whether his version of "The Lion and the Fox" appeared
as an exemplum within an invective, as did Archilochus's rendering of "The Eagle and the Fox" (see above, p. 14). Horace, for his
part, targets contemporaries only in very mildly mocking under-
tones at those points in his *Satires* and *Epistles* where he tells or

alludes to fables. A plagiarist named Celsus, for example, is reminded, as a friendly warning, of the jackdaw and his borrowed plumage (*Epistles* 1.3.15–20). Another fable, by contrast—"The Horse and the Man," the earliest extant text of which is found in Aristotle—is introduced by Horace in order to illustrate an argument from popular philosophy (*Epistles* 1.10.34–41 ~ *Aes.* 269a).

Conspicuously, three of the four fables which Horace actually tells in full as stories are embedded in reflections on his relations with Maecenas, his patron. Could it be that the fable is even being used here as a vehicle through which to express, in veiled form, unpleasant truths? In *Epistles* 1.17, which addresses Maecenas directly and includes Horace's version of "The Fox with the Swollen Belly" (vv. 29–33), muted criticism of the former is perceptible at every turn. But what about the context for the fable in *Satires* 2.3, where the poet seems instead to be making fun of himself? He has the other speaker in this dialogue berate him for a number of reasons, as, for instance, in 312–320:

> an, quodcumque facit Maecenas, te quoque verum est,
> tanto dissimilem et tanto certare minorem?
> absentis ranae pullis vituli pede pressis
> unus ubi effugit, matri denarrat, ut ingens
> belua cognatos eliserit: illa rogare,
> quantane? num tantum, sufflans se, magna fuisset?
> 'maior dimidio.' 'num tanto?' cum magis atque
> se magis inflaret, 'non, si te ruperis', inquit,
> 'par eris.' Haec a te non multum abludit imago.

Or is whatever Maecenas does all right for you too, who are so unlike him and far too insignificant to be a match? When the young ones of a frog, who happened to be away, had been squashed under the hoof of a calf and only one had escaped, it tells its mother how a big monster had crushed its brothers. She asks: "How big?" Had it been this big? she says, puffing herself up "Half as big again." "This big, then?" When she has blown herself up more and more, he says: "Even if you blow yourself to bursting, you'll never be the same size." This image is not so very unlike you.

Is Horace really just laughing at himself here? Or is this a little 'dig' in his patron's direction as well? Maecenas does in a certain sense expect him to "puff himself up." Some degree of inflation is, after all, inevitable if Augustus is to be glorified in the tones he, Maecenas, wants to hear—praises which, however, only represent but one part of the works of this poet, who values any opportunity to retreat from the world of politics.

Horace's version of "Town Mouse and Country Mouse" (*Satires* 2.6.79–117) also contains veiled criticism of Maecenas, even if readers through the ages have tended to overlook this in their delight at the artistry with which the genre piece was composed. Yet it really ought to have set them thinking, as one convention of this literary form is disregarded here: fables normally 'home in' on the lesson to be learnt, leaving out anything that is not strictly relevant. Moreover, in Horace's presentation of this exemplum the story proper is not followed by a "thus too . . ." introducing the moral (cf. *Epistles* 1.10.39: *sic*); instead the fable—and the satire—ends with the country mouse's parting words.

Even without an auctorial explanation the lesson seems clear: "country life is safer than town life." But does this platitude alone constitute the entire message of a poem which opens with a look at the sticky subject of patron-client relationships? A more obvious assumption would surely be that readers are supposed to interpolate an unspoken *sic et ego* after the country dweller's adieu, so that the poet can be seen to identify himself with the *mus rusticus* and Maecenas with the *mus urbanus*: "And thus I too, a freedman's son from a country town, find the life that you lead in Rome close to the Empire's nerve center overly dangerous." One particularly manifest hint that the town mouse is supposed to represent Maecenas can be found in the middle of the fable, when the wee beastie recommends making the short stay on earth a meaningful one by leading a merry life (vv. 94–97). Is this not the pseudo-Epicurean philosophy that a man like Maecenas could well be supposed to have shared? On the whole, however, such allusions to the real world are so well hidden under the mantle of fable that neither Maecenas nor anyone else can have taken umbrage. In the first section of our next chapter we shall be making the acquaintance of a Roman writer of verse fables who, although as skilled as Horace in the art of concealment, still fell foul of his masters.

* * *

There are two studies devoted specifically to fables used as exempla in Greek and Latin texts: Karadagli (1981) offers in her dissertation little more than a string of selected instances (some with a translation), but van Dijk's book (1997) must already be ranked as a standard work on the subject. It looks at texts dating from the archaic period through to the age of Hellenism, supplying an edition of each (442–568), and is soon to be continued with a volume on the imperial age (cf. the reviews by Gibbs 1998 and Holzberg 1998).

The beginnings of the Greek fable in archaic and classical times are considered by Thiele (1908), Nøjgaard (1964–1967, 1:442–463), Adrados (1979–1987, 1:381–420, and 1999a, 141–497), Lasserre (1984), West (1984), Jedrkiewicz (1987), and van Dijk (1997); the genre's Mesopotamian origins are discussed by Smend (1908), Diels (1910), Perry (1959, 25–28, and 1965, xxviii–xxxiv), La Penna (1964), Nøjgaard (1964–1967, 1:433–441), Koep (1969, 136–138), Adrados (1979–1987, 1:301–379, and 1999a, 287–366), Burkert (1984, 110–114), Falkowitz (1984), and Oettinger (1992).

On Hesiod's fable see especially Daly (1961b), Livrea (1970), West (1978, 3–15, 204–209), Lonsdale (1989), Leclerc (1992), Dalfen (1994–1995), and Hubbard (1995). The fables in Archilochus are treated by Bowra (1940), Adrados (1964), West (1974, 132–134, and 1982), and Janko (1980). Those fables in Aeschylus are discussed by Adrados (1965), West (1979), Davies (1981), and Nappa (1994). Herodotus's fable is discussed by Hirsch (1985–1986). On the fables in Aristophanes' *Wasps* see Rothwell (1995); on the fable in Plato's *Alcibiades* (1) see Desclos (1997); on the fables in Aristotle see Zinato (1989) and Narkiss (1995); and on those in Callimachus *Iambi* 4 see Castrucci (1996). The *testimonia* for Aesop's life are assembled in Perry (1952, 211–229) and examined by Hausrath (1909, 1707–1718), Chambry (1927, ix–xvii), Birch (1955), Perry (1965, xxxv–xlvi), Holbek (1977), Adrados (1979–1987, 1:286–298, and 1999a, 271–284), West (1984), Jedrkiewicz (1989, 41–68), Brodersen (1992), Luzzatto (1996a and 1996c), and Ragone (1997). For sociohistorical interpretations of the early Greek fable see Crusius (1913), Spoerri (1942–1943), Meuli (1954; cf. review by Perry 1957), La Penna (1961), Gual (1977), Schmidt (1979, 79–80), Cascajero (1991 and 1992), and Rothwell (1995). For useful reading on the definition of the genre see Bieber (1906, 2–10), Hausrath (1909, 1704–1706), Hofmann (1922), Wienert (1925, 5–25), Perry (1959, 17–25), Nøjgaard (1964–1967, 1:23–129), Adrados (1979–1987,

1:17–59, and 1999a, 17–47), Wissemann (1992), and van Dijk (1993, 1995a, and 1997, 1–115; cf. ibid. the edition of all ancient *testimonia* for the fable: 400–441). The use of formulaic language in fables is discussed by Fraenkel (1924), Perry (1940, 395–400), Nøjgaard (1964–1967, 1:142 ff.), and Karadagli (1981, 97–139).

The contents and purpose of the *repertorium* compiled by Demetrius of Phalerum are considered by Wehrli (1949, 67–68), Perry (1953 and 1962), Nøjgaard (1964–1967, 1:467–468, 1:477–478), and Adrados (1979–1987, 1:421–508, and 1999a, 410–497). *Papyrus Rylands 493*, published in Roberts (1938) and in *CFA* 1.2.187–189 (there only the legible parts), is examined by Perry in Oldfather (1940, 216–218), Perry (1940, 396–397, 400–401, 409–411), Adrados (1952, 1979–1987, 1:67–73, and 1999a, 54–60), and Nøjgaard (1964–1967, 1:492–508). A late-second-century papyrus possibly contains another fragment from a fable *repertorium:* in *PColon. II.64* (first edited in Kramer and Hagedorn 1978, 56–61; cf. also Karadagli 1981, 37–38) a man tells a fable that corresponds to *Aes.* 480 and begins (only the first sentence survives) another one ("The Ram and the Ape," which is not in *Aes.*).

A survey of the Greek fables used as exempla by authors from the imperial age can be found in Bieber (1906) and Hausrath (1938, 1487–1493); cf. also Davies (1987) and van Dijk (1996). On the use of fables in rhetoric schools of the period see Hausrath (1898, 312–314) and Marrou (1957, 252–254). The papyrus fragments of fable texts written down by students are accessible in the following editions: the *Tabulae Assendelftianae* (first edited by Hesseling 1892–1893)—with the exception of those texts taken from Babrius (cf. Luzzatto and La Penna 1986, xxx)—in Crusius (1897, 234) and in *CFA* 1.2.117–119; *PMichigan 457* (first edited by Sanders 1947) in Roberts (1957); *POxy. 1404* (first edited by Grenfell and Hunt 1915) and *PAmherst II.26* (first edited by Grenfell and Hunt 1901) in Cavenaile (1958, 117–120) (cf. here Ihm 1902, Radermacher 1902, 142–145, and Della Corte 1966); and *PGrenfell II.84* (first edition: Grenfell and Hunt 1897) in *CFA* 1.2.119 (cf. Oldfather 1929). Recent papyrus discoveries are described in Adrados (1999b); on the use of fables as school texts see Fisher (1987). The fables of Ps.-Dositheus are published in Goetz (1892, 39–47) and (the Greek text only) in *CFA* 1.2.120–129; cf. also the fragment *PSI 848* (first edited in 1925) and Cavenaile

(1958, 118). For a discussion of Ps.-Dositheus, see Getzlaff (1907), Nøjgaard (1964–1967, 2.402–403), and Adrados (1979–1987, 2.213–225, and 2000, 221–235). Aphthonius's fables—text in Sbordone (1932) and *CFA* 1.2.133–151—are examined in Adrados (1979–1987, 2.227–242, and 2000, 236–253).

Bieber (1906) and Hausrath (1938, 1487,1493–1494) give a survey of fables used as exempla by Roman authors. On the fable in Ennius see Müller (1976), Menna (1983), Cozzoli (1995), and Del Vecchio and Fiore (1998); on the fables in Lucilius see Cozzoli (1995), and on the fable in Catullus see La Penna (1997); the fables in Horace are discussed by Della Corte (1986), Holzberg (1991a), Warmuth (1992), Fedeli (1993), Adrados (1994), and Cozzoli (1995), and the fable in Livy by Schmidt (1979, 74–79), Peil (1985), Havas (1989), and Hillgruber (1996).

2

Fable Books in Verse

■ **Phaedrus,** *Fabulae Aesopiae*

Although we cannot definitely rule out the possibility that Babrius lived and wrote before Phaedrus, all the evidence does suggest that it was the Roman and not the Greek who wrote the first ancient book of poetry to consist of verse fables. His *Liber primus fabularum Aesopiarum* was published some time during the first thirty-odd years of the first century A.D., and what certainly is specifically Roman is the author's association with the tradition of Augustan poetry. Formal and thematic linking of *carmina*—and thus the creation in book-rolls of the "garland of song"—had been developed by the Augustan poets into an art previously unparalleled in ancient literature. How Phaedrus set about emulating his great predecessors in this respect is unfortunately a question of guesswork for us now, since the five *libri* which finally constituted his fable book have survived in fragments only. The division into *libri* is retained in one of the few Phaedrus manuscripts we possess, the *Codex Pithoeanus,* but the five book texts offered in it must be abridged editions of the originals, at least as far as books 2–5 are concerned. First, these are not as long as a *liber* normally would be: while book 1 does comprise thirty-one fables, book 2 only has eight, book 3, nineteen, book 4, twenty-six, and book 5, ten. Second, a fifteenth-century selection of fables from books 2–5 compiled by the Italian humanist Niccolò Perotti includes, besides a number of texts also found in books 2–5 of the

Pithoeanus version, thirty-two not found there. The arrangement of this anthology—now known as the *Appendix Perottina*—allows no conclusions as to the original position of the thirty-two fables within the four *libri*.

At least one fable must also have been left out of Phaedrus's first book as it stands in the *Pithoeanus* edition. In his prologue to the *liber primus* the poet apologizes, as it were, for letting trees talk (v. 6), but there are none to be heard in said codex. It seems probable, in fact, that more than one text was omitted in the *Pithoeanus* abridgment of book 1, given the contents of another fable manuscript: the *Codex Vossianus lat. 8° 15* (Leiden University Library). This contains a collection copied around 1025 by Ademar of Chabannes at St. Martial, Limoges; the text comprises prose adaptations of Phaedrian fables belonging to the fourth-century *Aesopus Latinus*, together with a further thirty fables based directly on Phaedrus. These latter are not adaptations, but the results of mechanical prose 'deconstruction' of the original verse; nineteen of them can be matched to texts in the *Codex Pithoeanus*, leaving eleven for which no corresponding fable can be found there (4, 13, 18, 34, 35, 36, 37, 38, 43, 58, 60 = 4, 15, 22, 41, 51, 84, 53, 54, 63, 82, 92 Th. ~ Aes. 384, 352, 150, 181, 563–566, 153, 571, 137). The Phaedrian origins of these eleven are, however, so evident that there can be no doubt as to their source. The nineteen prose paraphrases of which the original poems have survived all prove to be versions of fables from book 1 of Phaedrus, while the verse texts turned into the *Aesopus Latinus* prose adaptations are scattered over all five books of the *Fabulae Aesopiae* and the *Appendix*. It is reasonable to assume, therefore, that only poems from book 1 were turned into the prose paraphrases we find in the *Ademar Codex*, and that the eleven fables we only know in that form also originally stood in book 1, which would in that case once have comprised some forty fables or more.

If this is true—and it is certainly plausible—then the first book of Phaedrus's fables as found in the *Codex Pithoeanus* is also a much-abridged version. Nevertheless, the arrangement of the thirty-one fables it does offer still conveys a certain impression of the structural form given by Phaedrus to at least one of his books. We may assume, to begin with, that the two fables following the brief prologue to book 1 and the two now counted as numbers 30 and 31 originally formed a framework for the *liber,* since numbers 1–2 and 30–31 deal with each of the two themes addressed several times within the book: cruelty of the stronger toward the weaker, and ordinary people in the face of superior powers. "The Wolf and the Lamb" (1 ~ *Aes.* 155), based on a Greek source, finds its counterpart in "The Kite and the Doves" (31), a fable only known to us from Phaedrus. "The Frogs Ask for a King" (2 ~ *Aes.* 44), again based on a Greek λόγος, is matched by "The Frogs Dread the Battle of the Bulls" (30), another story we only know from the Roman author. The four poems thus form two pairs set in chiastic arrangement (*abba*), and one such observation promptly leads to another: there are more pairs of poems within the book. We find thematically linked fable couples either right next to each other or separated by a number of other poems, and their connection lies either in an analogy between them (e.g., 18 and 19; 4 and 20) or in an antithesis (e.g., 16 and 17; 5 and 21).

Phaedrus possibly intended the structural link between the second and the penultimate fable of book 1 as a reminiscence of the similar link in Horace's first book of *Odes* between the second and the penultimate poem. In *Odes* 1.2 the speaker, grumbling about the Civil War, wonders: "Whom will Jupiter charge with the task of avenging this outrage?" (vv. 29–30); in Phaedrus 1.2 the frogs, to which the fable's narrator, "Aesop," compares the Athenians and their civil unrest, ask Jupiter for a king. Horace's penultimate poem in *Odes* 1 (*carmen* 31) refers to Octavian's victory over Antony and Cleopatra at Actium, and the penultimate fable in Phaedrus's *liber primus* to the battle *de principatu* among the bulls. One argument for interpreting these similarities as a deliberate allusion to Horace is that, of all the Augustan poets, he is the one on whom Phaedrus models himself most closely in terms of form and content. This becomes particularly clear in the prologues and epilogues, where the fabulist articulates his perception of himself as a poet. We find there, for example, the combined agenda *risum movere* and *consilio monere* (1. *prol.* 3–4), which corresponds to Horace's blend of *ridere* with *dicere verum,* and *prodesse* with *delectare* (*Satires* 1.1.24; *Ars poetica* 333). It is Phaedrus's avowed intention not to brand (*notare*) individuals with his satire (3. *prol.* 49–50 ~ Hor. *Satires* 1.4.5), and he too, in a poem addressing his patron, contrasts the latter's lifestyle with his own (3. *prol.*

1 ff.; cf. Hor. *Odes* 3.29). Phaedrus also claims to have a special bond with the Muses (cf. 3. *prol.* 17 ff. and Hor. *Odes* 3.4.1 ff.) and, finally, is just as confident that fame will come to him (3. *prol.* 61 ~ Hor. *Odes* 3.30.6–7).

Remembering that, prior to the publication of the *libri fabularum Aesopiarum,* the fable did not count as a genuine literary genre, but was simply seen as a means to an end, we ought to ask whether Rome's 'Aesop' is being serious when he proudly places himself in the same league as one of the greatest Latin poets. Before trying to answer this, we must first examine Phaedrus's formal skills and his intentions.

In order to determine how the poet handled his stylistic and metrical 'tools' for the composition of his verse fables, let us look at one example, "The Crow and the Fox" (1.13 ~ *Aes.* 124):

> *Qui se laudari gaudet verbis subdolis,*
> *Fere dat poenas turpi paenitentia.*
> *Cum de fenestra corvus raptum caseum*
> *Comesse vellet, celsa residens arbore,*
> 5   *Vulpes hunc vidit, deinde sic coepit loqui:*
> *'O qui tuarum, corve, pennarum est nitor!*
> *Quantum decoris corpore et vultu geris!*
> *Si vocem haberes, nulla prior ales foret.'*
> *At ille stultus, dum vult vocem ostendere,*
> 10   *Emisit ore caseum, quem celeriter*
> *Dolosa vulpes avidis rapuit dentibus.*
> *Tunc demum ingemuit corvi deceptus stupor.*

He who enjoys being praised in words that are false usually pays the price in shamed repentance. When a crow, settled on a high tree, was about to eat some cheese he had thieved from a window, a fox saw him and then began to speak as follows: "O, what a sheen there is to your feathers, Crow! What grace you show in body and countenance! If you had the voice, no bird would come before you!" Thereupon that fool, determined to demonstrate his voice, let the cheese fall from his mouth; this the cunning fox swiftly snatched with his greedy fangs. Only then did the crow, in its stupidity outwitted, start to wail.

Like a number of Phaedrus's fables, this one is symmetrical in structure. The *promythium* (vv. 1–2) and the author's closing remark

(12)—together three lines—frame the actual narrative, which falls into three sections with, again, three lines each: exposition (3–5), action proper, that is, the fox's speech (6–8), and outcome (9–11). The two forms of *rapere* (3 *raptum,* 11 *rapuit*) and the parallel use of enjambment in 3–4 and 10–11 create an inner framework around the narrative, and the fox's speech—three consecutive sentences, each taking up exactly one line—thus gains particular prominence as the centerpiece.

In the exposition two verses introduce the crow, while only one is devoted to the fox. There is method in this: in order to prepare the ground for the crow's portrayal as vain fool, Phaedrus uses alliteration with *c*'s (all pronounced as *k*'s) to produce a penetrating racket, and this needs a longer period for more effect. In addition, the word *residens* is given special metrical emphasis. Its first syllable stands at a point in the iambic *senarius*—the meter used by Phaedrus in his fables—where one would normally expect a long vowel; instead two short ones appear (*rĕsĭ-*), with which the poet draws the reader's attention to the crow's 'throning' position. For the preliminary characterization of the fox as a fast mover, by contrast, just one verse (5) is enough, and the alliterative *v*'s there help to make it reminiscent of another quick worker's famous *veni vidi vici.*

The fox's speech is brief but packed with rhetorical figures, so that the effectiveness of the words seems entirely credible. In verse 6, for example, the double hyperbaton *qui tuarum* and *pennarum . . . nitor* are wrapped around *corve,* and thus the word order shows us the crow enwrapped, as it were, in the glossiness of its feathers. And, just as the flattery is intensified in three stages, the vocabulary involved is stepped up from *qui* to *quantum* to the speech's four-word crowning touch, *nulla prior ales foret,* where, in addition, two words are given particular emphasis: *prior,* with its two short vowels, is metrically irregular, and *ales* is a term otherwise found primarily in poetry of more elevated content.

In the third section of the narrative, the first half features the crow, the other the fox (*At . . . caseum, quem . . . dentibus*). The swift vulpine reactions already hinted at in verse 5 are accentuated here by, for example, the three metrical feet in which the poet substitutes two short vowels for one long (*cĕlĕriter . . . ăvĭdis rắpŭit*). The final auctorial remark on the crow's behavior adds a touch of irony, with its deliberately affected choice of expression: *ingemuit corvi deceptus stupor* (literally: "groan did then the crow's deceived foolishness"). This imitation of Homeric diction—as found, for example, in *Odyssey* 16.476: "Then did smile the sacred might of Telemachus"—lends the crow something of a character from a mock-heroic epic.

To sum up briefly our observations on typical features of Phaedrus's style and meter: the poet uses mainly *sermo urbanus*, for which the iambic *senarius*, on account of its close proximity to the everyday language of educated Romans, is the most suitable meter. For comic effect, however, he occasionally throws in something more 'highfalutin' which he, the author of 'minor' poems, likes to take from the grander diction of 'major' poetry. His fables are carefully structured, and he frequently uses rhetorical figures; these are not, as was once often maintained, purely ornamental and void of function, but serve as strategic devices for underlining the *fabula docet*. To the same end, the poet regularly admits the resolution of long syllables; this is particularly striking because, in the construction of his iambic *senarii*, Phaedrus does not take as many liberties as the Roman comedians Plautus and Terence.

"The Crow and the Fox" is a fable which was certainly familiar in Greece and Rome well before Phaedrus published his poems. Horace refers to the story (*Satires* 2.5.55–56), and this documents its existence before the first century A.D. The question arises, therefore, as to Phaedrus's possible source or sources. He himself indicates at the beginning of his prologue to book 1 that he has turned prose fables into verse: "I have polished in *senarii* the *materia* which *Aesopus auctor* invented." By "Aesop" Phaedrus probably means a Hellenistic *repertorium* like the one found in *Papyrus Rylands 493*, as the following observation—made by Perry (1940)—would seem to suggest. Although in a book of verse fables the moral to be gleaned from each story could either be presented as an *epimythium* at the end of each poem or, equally well, as a *promythium* at the beginning, Phaedrus displays a noticeable preference in his *liber primus* for the *promythium*. He uses it there twenty-five times—including the example considered above (1.13.1–2)—and in only four poems does he choose the *epimythium.* In all his other *libri,* by contrast, the ratio is considerably more balanced, and so we may infer that he used a fable book which, like the texts in the *Rylands* papyrus, only contained *promythia,* the form which provided the entries for the 'subject index' required in *promptuaria.* In his adaptation of these fables Phaedrus would have frequently imitated their original structure in the course of his *liber primus,* but perhaps decided from book 2 onward to move the *fabula docet* more often to the end of the poem.

The second book also sees the start of a series of auctorial remarks which reveal that Phaedrus is gradually casting off his source, "Aesop." These begin in the prologue with a request that the reader now look kindly upon the poet's personal additions to that which is purely "Aesopic," and they continue through to the prologue in book 5, where the poet declares that any further mention of the name *Aesopus* merely represents a 'marketing strategy' for his own new products. And indeed the texts in books 1–5 of our abridged Phaedrus, the *Codex Pithoeanus,* together with those in the *Appendix Perottina* seem to corroborate this. Apart from forty-eight fables which other ancient authors also knew in some form and which, therefore, could have stood in Phaedrus's source, we find there a total of sixty-eight which he alone tells (cf. the critical apparatus in Guaglianone 1969). A few of these could perhaps have been adapted by Phaedrus from the "Aesopus" he used and simply were never retold by any other ancient author known to us. It seems much more likely, however, that Phaedrus created the majority of them himself, either by modifying motifs he had found in Greek Aesopica or by taking his inspiration from texts that belonged to quite different literary genres and thus creating entirely new fables.

One motif from a fable, for example, was probably developed by Phaedrus into the erotic tale which stands as number 15 in the *Appendix Perottina.* The story: a widow incarcerates herself in the tomb where her husband's body lies, and this demonstration of chaste virtue makes her famous. A soldier on guard-duty nearby, his mission being to prevent the bodies of crucified criminals from being taken down and buried by their bereaved families, manages to seduce her anyway. When a body vanishes during one of their nocturnal trysts, the widow offers her lover the corpse of her husband as substitute. Scholars are generally convinced that this *fabliau* is a faithful rendering of a now-lost Hellenistic source, but only because they are more comfortable with this assumption. After all, the alternative would be to suggest that Petronius owed the material for his celebrated novella *The Widow of Ephesus* (*Satyrica* 111–112) to Phaedrus, an author not usually held by classicists to be particularly original. However, M. Massaro (1981a) detects several allusions in Phaedrus's version to Ovid, for example, to verses from the Lucretia legend in the *Fasti* (2.721 ff.), to a *praeceptum* from the *Ars amatoria* (2.345–348 ~ *Appendix Perottina* 15.20–24), and to the *militia amoris* and *amator exclusus* imagery commonly used in Roman elegy. Phaedrus's intentions in 'citing' all this quite obviously have something to do with parody, and it therefore seems conceivable that a Greek motif—one which is tangible for us in chapter 129 of the second/third-century *Aesop Romance*, but was undoubtedly not told there for the first time—was being transplanted here onto Roman territory by the poet, who at the same time decided to intensify the misogynist element. The motif as we know it would have offered Phaedrus this much: a peasant has his oxen stolen while he is busy seducing a widow in mourning at her husband's tomb.

Many of the fables known to us only from Phaedrus display one striking difference when compared to his versions of "Aesopic" texts, especially to those in book 1: in the former, that is, the Phaedriana, the pleasure which the author derives from narrating is often dominant, relegating any didactic intentions to the wings. In clear contrast to this, many of the fables which are adaptations of λόγοι Αἰσώπειοι betray Phaedrus's efforts to heighten his readers' awareness of certain problems: of the trouble, that is, which arises when the weak clash with the strong, or when ordinary folk become personally entangled with the established powers. We have, of course, no way of knowing to what extent the Greek "Aesop" used by Phaedrus was already interested in such issues. A number of the fables which, in the form given to them by Phaedrus, indicate deep concern for social and moral questions are, however, also available to us in other versions—by Babrius and by the author of the *Collectio Augustana*. A comparison of the three adaptations produces in each case the same results: only the Roman author signals—simply in the way he tells the story—that he condemns the strong who exploit their advantage over the weak, and only the Roman author describes as graphically as possible how dangerous it always is for ordinary people to take on the powers that be.

The very first fable in book 1 of the *Fabulae Aesopiae* serves as a good example here. There the wolf comes up with various arguments which would justify gobbling up the lamb; his intended victim refutes these one by one, but in the end is gobbled up anyway. Neither in the version by Babrius (89), nor in the corresponding *Collectio Augustana* text (*Aes.* 155) do the narrators try, be it with one single word, to cast the wolf in a negative light and thus arouse sympathy for the lamb. In the *Augustana* text, moreover, the fable ends with the wolf saying a few words which merely indicate that he is about to consume the lamb—the dirty deed itself takes place 'offstage.' In Phaedrus, on the other hand, the canine "bandit" (4: *latro*) approaches the lamb with "his reprobate muzzle" (3: *fauce improba*), then after their exchange "pounces upon the lamb and tears it to pieces in an unjustifiable killing" (13: *correptum lacerat iniusta nece*), although the lamb, "terrified" (6: *timens*), had been able to invalidate all his reasoning "with the potency of truth" (9: *veritatis viribus*; note the alliteration!).

Comparing briefly Phaedrus's "The Frog and the Cow" (1.24) and "Town Mouse and Country Mouse" (this can be reconstructed from the *Ademar Codex* 13 = 15 Th.) with Horace's version of each (supra, pp. 34–35), we observe how dismal Phaedrus thinks the prospects are for the lowly or poor who want to compete with the mighty or rich. In Horace the fable of the mother frog who tries to puff herself up to the size of an *ingens belua* ends, as we saw above, with her being told that she will never match the beast in size, not even if she blows herself up to bursting (*Satires* 2.3.319–320). In Phaedrus the frog really does burst, but this is no longer the irony of an Epicurean sage—it is an earnest warning of mortal danger. The perils facing the country mouse in town do not escape the narrator of the fable in Horace's *Satires* 2.6.111 ff. Only Phaedrus, however, introduces the following motif into the scene where the two mice are disturbed during their feast in an urban villa: while the country mouse runs round along the walls in fear of its life (*mortemque metuens circa* [Phaedrus: probably *per*] *parietes cursitat*), the "smart" townie slips into its hole. Everything is duck soup for the rich.

Fables like the three just considered virtually cry out for us to track down possible allusions in the picture of life presented to the author's own sphere. Such a search requires, of course, some knowledge of Phaedrus's actual circumstances, but reliable information is in lamentably short supply. We know that he was born in Greece, became a slave in the service of Augustus, and was later manumitted by the emperor. By A.D. 31 he had published the first two books of his *Fabulae Aesopiae*, which caused him to fall in some way foul of Sejanus, the formidable Prefect of the Praetorian guard under Tiberius. Later he also brought out books 3–5, dedicating them to his (otherwise unknown) patrons Eutychus, Particulo, and Philetus. Phaedrus probably died at a fairly advanced age around the middle of the first century. Looking for connections between the poet's personal experiences and the way in which the "Aesopic" material selected by him is handled, scholars have in the past tended to overshoot the mark, reading the fables as coded texts and extracting from them new biographical 'facts.' The most enterprising of such 'decoders' is A. de Lorenzi (1955), in whose 214-page book speculation on the life and times of the *libertus Augusti* is rampant; we have, in effect, been furnished here with a "Phaedrus Romance" to match the ancient *Aesop Romance*. For a sociohistorical interpretation of the fables this method was, however, as unfruitful as the attempts then variously made to filter from the words of the poet the voice of the former slave: in the 1960s and 1970s this reading revealed a Phaedrus who seemingly used his poems to incite Rome's oppressed masses to rebellion.

Admittedly, at one oft-quoted point in his prologue to book 3, Phaedrus does indeed offer an explanation for the invention of the fable that would seem to justify such interpretations. The slave (i.e., Aesop), he says, being subject to the arbitrary power of others, did not dare to speak openly and so 'translated' his personal thoughts and feelings into the language of fables; he could thus playfully avoid vilification and accusations by making up amusing stories (33–37). But nowhere in Phaedrus's fables are ordinary folk encouraged to defy the authorities. On the contrary, they are advised repeatedly to accept things as they are, and this for the first time in the very second fable of book 1. Here some frogs who enjoy the freedom of the swamp ask Jupiter to send them a king, complain about the plank accordingly enthroned, but must then live (or rather die) in dread of the water snake that succeeds it. What the fable is telling us is that when order has been restored by a monarch to a state previously in anarchic turmoil, bowing to this authority is a lesser evil than demanding a new government; after all, the monarch's replacement could turn out to be a tyrannical fiend who slaughters his fellow citizens. This same message runs through Phaedrus's fables like a leitmotif wherever something simply and immutably is what it is: learn to live with it.

The conformist ideology voiced by Phaedrus on a political and social level is accompanied, however, by relentless criticism of contemporary morals. He may state at the outset that he does not intend to target individuals, but that he wants quite generally "to display life itself and the ways of men and women" (3. *prol.* 50: *ipsam vitam et mores hominum ostendere*). Nevertheless, his criticism is—as the texts discussed above reveal—frequently directed at typical members of the property-owning elite. The *epimythium* of the very first fable, "The Wolf and the Lamb," explains that the tale was written for those people "who oppress the innocent on trumped-up pretexts" (1.1.15), and in first-century Roman society the rich would be more likely to take this as a reference to their kind than the poor. Furthermore, at a time when the *principatus* was first showing signs of becoming a *dominatio,* fear of opposition to the system and its supporters was steadily growing. It is therefore hardly surprising that the one or the other powerful Roman suspected that he would be identified with the one or the other figure exposed by Phaedrus to ridicule, and so made trouble for the author, as, according to Phaedrus himself (3. *prol.* 41 ff.), Sejanus did. However, there is little point in combing through the fables for allusions to then-contemporaries because we do not know today who, for example, might have been one of those *qui fictis causis innocentes opprimunt.* If Phaedrus—in spite of his assurances to the contrary—was actually targeting specific individuals with any of his broadsides, then he will doubtlessly have camouflaged this so well that even his coevals would have trouble identifying them.

One form of camouflage—and this brings us back finally to the question raised earlier in the chapter—is perhaps the proud opinion Phaedrus seems to have of his own worth as a poet, a perception which, at first glance, appears distinctly odd. The discrepancy between, on the one hand, the lofty aspirations of a writer who sees himself on a par with the Augustan poets and, on the other, this same writer's concentration exclusively on the themes of lighter poetry—subjects generally considered low-brow—could be explained as follows: Phaedrus himself assumes that, if he stresses the serious nature of his poetry's message in such a paradoxical fashion, his readers will laugh and be even less likely to take him seriously. This means, however, that he can simply use truth to disguise truth, as it were. And only readers who can see through this trick will appreciate that the substance of Phaedrus's fables is as profoundly significant as the wisdom camouflaged by the fool with cap and bells.

* * *

The history of Phaedrus studies, outlined in Holzberg (1991b), was documented in regular surveys prior to the Second World War (Heydenreich 1884–1888, Draheim 1889–1925, Port 1933–1939), and later only in one report for the years 1969–1974 (Tortora 1975), but the exhaustive bibliography by Lamb (1998) does list all literature published since 1596. Guaglianone (1969) offers the best critical edition (cf., however, Nøjgaard 1972 and Önnerfors 1987); the prose paraphrases from the *Ademar Codex* are published in Thiele (1905 and 1910) and Zander (1921), who both try to reconstruct the original wording. Perry (1965) provides an English prose translation, and Luzzatto (1976) supplies a stopgap for the definitive commentary yet to be written; Oberg (2000) does not offer notes on single words, phrases, and so forth (and thus includes few points of language or style), but presents instead (for a wider readership) interpretations of the individual fables. For indices see Cinquini (1905) and Cremona (1980); on the textual history (summarized succinctly in Önnerfors 1987), compare especially Robert (1893), Zwierlein (1970), Finch (1971a and 1971b), Gatti (1979), and Boldrini (1988, 1990a–c, and 1991a–b).

Henderson (1999) tries to reconstruct the original contents and structure of the *Corpus Phaedrianum;* his article, which is also a brilliant contribution to our appreciation of Phaedrus's significance within the context of literary history, appears to be the revised version of a chapter from his unpublished Cambridge thesis of 1977 (on which cf. Lamb 1998, 113, no. 1034). The best general studies and broader views are Duff (1927), Schanz and Hosius (1935), Hausrath (1938), Perry (1965, lxxiii–cii), Nøjgaard (1964–1967, 2:15–188), Grubmüller (1977, 52–56), Currie (1984), Adrados (1979–1987, 2:125–171, and 2000, 121–174), Riedel (1989, 194–212), and Jedrkiewicz (1990). Phaedrus's language and style are discussed by Craven (1973), Massaro (1979 and 1981b), Pugliarello (1981–1982), and Moretti (1982), and his metrics by Guaglianone (1968), Korzeniewski (1970), and Barabino (1981). Perry (1940 and 1962) offers some important ideas as to Phaedrus's possible sources. Comparisons between Phaedrian fables and other Aesopica are drawn by Thiele (1906–1911), Weinreich (1931), and Hausrath (1936)—all three of whom have a rather low opinion of Phaedrus's narrative talents—later also by Pisi (1977; cf. Luzzatto 1979). De Lorenzi (1955) relies heavily on speculation for his reconstruction of Phaedrus's vita, whilst Önnerfors (1987) provides a valuable account of the known facts. Phaedrus's own conception of himself as poet is discussed by Dams (1970, 96–113), Lamberti (1980), Koster (1991), Bernardi Perini (1992), Wissemann (1992), and Bloomer (1997, 102–107). Aspects of sociohistorical interpretation are treated by Christes (1979), Schmidt (1979), de Maria (1987), Olshausen (1995), Oberg (1996b), and Bloomer (1997; cf. esp. 75: "A successful reading depends on the reader's granting the poet his due status"); on thematic traditions see Oberg (1997 and 1999). The following interpretations of specific fables merit particular mention: on 1.1, Nøjgaard (1979 and 1984) and Küppers (1990); on 1.2, Zwierlein (1989); on 1.5, Tartuferi (1984); on 1.15, Olshausen (1995); on 1.29, Bertini (1981); on 3.7, Küppers (1990); on 3.12, Speckenbach (1978); on 4.26, Bellonzi (1973); on 5.8, Bajoni (1999); on *Appendix Perottina* 15, Müller (1980), Massaro (1981a), and Huber (1990, 67–82); on "Town Mouse and Country Mouse" (*Ademar* 13 = 15 Th.), Holzberg 1991a; see also Henderson (2001) for his readings of various Phaedriana. Heintze (1989) identifies the remains of a relief on marble as those of a stela for Phaedrus's tomb, but the theory is highly conjectural.

* * *

■ Babrius, *Mythiambi Aesopei*

Whether Phaedrus was aware that, by writing 'iambic' fables, he was in a sense continuing the tradition of Archilochus, Semonides, and Callimachus is a question we cannot answer. Babrius, on the other hand, who composed his *Fables in Iambics* sometime between the end of the first and the beginning of the third century, seems to have been following consciously in, if no one else's, Callimachus's footsteps. Not only was he, like the Alexandrian poet, attached to a court—we shall be returning to this below—but he also chose for his fables a meter which, as far as we know, Callimachus was the first to use for the genre: the *choliambus*, or scazon. This 'limping' verse form occurs in the Hellenistic author's *Iambi* 2 and 4, which each center on a fable: "How Man Came to Be Loquacious" (frag. 192 Pfeiffer = *Aes.* 431), and "The Laurel and the Olive" (frag. 194 Pfeiffer = *Aes.* 439).

Babrius was apparently even thinking specifically of one of these two fables when he wrote the prologue to his first book of *Mythiambi*. Callimachus talks in *Iambi* 2 of an age in which the animals had still possessed the power of speech, and it is this same age that Babrius defines in his prologue as "golden": a time when all living creatures could converse with one another, when gods and humans were on the best of terms. The fairy-tale world of the *aetas aurea* is, then, the setting Babrius picks for his characters, and an explanation for this choice is hinted at in the last three lines of the prologue. There (17–19) he tells the poems' addressee, a prince called Branchus:

> ὧν (sc. μύθων) νῦν ἕκαστον ἀνθίσας ἐμῇ μνήμῃ
> μελισταγές σοι νοῦ τὸ κηρίον θήσω,
> πικρῶν ἰάμβων σκληρὰ κῶλα θηλ<ύνας>.

And now I shall adorn each of those fables with the flowers of my own Muse. I shall set before you a poetical honeycomb, as it were, dripping with sweetness, having softened the hard chords of the stinging iambic.

What he means is clearly this: that although the *choliambus* was once—especially in Greece's archaic literature, but to a certain extent in Callimachus too—the meter of invective, he, Babrius, does not now see the fables he has written in this same metrical form as a vehicle for social and moral criticism. Instead, he has used the fable material as a basis for poetry that is free of topical allusions and is at the same time aesthetically pleasing.

Babrius's verse fables do indeed number among the most important works of post-Hellenistic Greek poetry, which makes it all the more regrettable that this fable book too survives in fragments only. Of the 144 reasonably complete fable texts presented in the most recent edition of Babrius (Luzzatto and La Penna 1986), we find only the first 123 in the one extant manuscript we can assume to be based on an ancient edition (*Codex A*). In this codex—which, incidentally, was not discovered until 1842 in a monastery on Mount Athos—the majority of fables from Babrius's second book are missing. A mere 21 of its estimated 80 original texts survive in other sources—the Leiden wax tablets (supra, p. 29), Ps.-Dositheus's *Hermeneumata* (see above, pp. 30–31), and two Byzantine collections (*Codd. G* and *V*). Fortunately we have, as in the case of Phaedrus, one further textual source: prose renderings of verse fables. For her Babrius edition M. J. Luzzatto managed to reconstruct fragments of the original poems from 21 such paraphrases, thus affording us a certain impression of the way in which the Greek author handled the fable material he had selected.

In the *Codex Athous* and in the collections *G* and *V,* the fables are ordered alphabetically according to the first letter in each. The assumption has frequently been that this arrangement cannot represent the original order of the poems, but must be the editorial contribution of a Byzantine schoolmaster. Only M. Nøjgaard (1964–1967) considers the possibility that the composition of fable books whose structure relies on the Greek alphabet could in fact represent a very ancient tradition. In his discussion of the *Collectio Augustana,* in which the fables also appear in the alphabetical order of their first letters, Nøjgaard notes that the animal proverbs in Sumerian collections from the second millennium B.C. were grouped according to their first character (this denoted in each case the animal involved), and that in both Babrius and in the *Collectio Augustana* a great many fables begin with the bare name of an animal, that is, no definite article is used (1:511–513). Nevertheless, Nøjgaard does not believe either that the order of the fables in the *Codex Athous* represents the original arrangement. The second prologue, he argues (2:351), separates quite randomly the poems A to Λ from the series beginning with M (and ending in the extant text with O).

If Babrius did order his fables alphabetically—and Nøjgaard's explanation of this structural principle makes it seem not entirely improbable—then we would, admittedly, expect to find the complete alphabet in each of the two books. Given that the second prologue begins with M, the most obvious conclusion even seems to be that a later editor rearranged all of Babrius's poems to form one alphabetical series, inserting the second prologue at the 'proper' place. And yet could we not just as easily conclude that it had been Babrius's intention to start with one book-roll containing fables which represented, by virtue of the first letter appearing in each, the first half of the Greek alphabet? True, this half would normally include the M's. It is striking, however, that the first book in the *Codex Athous* ends with nine fables featuring a lion (95, 97–99, 102, 103, 105–107)—striking because the 'king of beasts,' as we shall see below, plays an important role in the fabulous world which Babrius uses to mirror the real one. Let us suppose for a minute that Babrius deliberately rounded off his first book of *Mythiambi* with Λ-for-lion fables. M for Μῦθος ("fable") at the beginning of the second prologue would then make a good deal of sense as an initial for the second half of a two-book concept, this part to start with M-fables.

This hypothesis would seem to be supported by another observation. While alphabetical order is by no means strictly the rule in the *Codex Athous*, it is adhered to very consistently in one of the two Byzantine collections which contain fables by Babrius, *Codex G*, and similarly in another manuscript, *Ba*, which offers us paraphrases of Babrian texts (cf. the synopsis in Luzzatto and La Penna 1986, lxv–lxvii). Clearly these collections were ironing out the 'errors' presumed to have been made in the *recensio* represented now by the *Codex Athous*, but in reality not made at all. It was instead probably the poet himself who introduced a certain latitude into the system which he was borrowing from a very ancient tradition of book composition. He could thus allow himself, here and there at least, to order his fables according to subject matter as well. One example: in the *Codex Athous* fables 39 (*Δε-* after *Δρ-*) and 40 (*Διε-* before *Δια-*) form a pair because they both voice a political moral in the *epimythium*—something only rarely occurring in the rest of the work.

Babrius is, as already indicated above, much less interested in the didactic possibilities of the fable than he is in the scope it offers for narrating. In many of his poems he is clearly at great pains to create a graphic account, to describe the setting in detail, and to portray the figures involved as lifelike characters. In doing so he occasionally ventures beyond the narrative borders prescribed for the genre, so that, in comparison with other authors' versions of the same material, some of his fables seem more like skillfully developed short stories. Since this is best illustrated with an example, let us consider Babrius's poem about the donkey that wants to be a pet (129) and the version of this fable found in the *Collectio Augustana* (*Aes.* 91). The latter text is written in such simple prose that a translation will suffice here:

There was a man who owned a Maltese lapdog and a donkey, and he was forever playing with the dog. And whenever he dined out, he would bring something home for the dog and toss this to it when it beleaguered him, wagging its tail. Now, the donkey became jealous, rushed over too, and jumped up, kicking the man with its hooves. Then he became angry, ordered the donkey to be beaten, led away, and tied to its manger. The fable shows that not everyone has the same aptitude.

This text displays the tripartite structure familiar from many of the archaic and classical Greek fables (see above, p. 20) and from Phaedrus's version of "The Crow and the Fox" (1.13, supra).

Let us now see how Babrius handles the fable:

> Ὄνον τις ἔτρεφε καὶ κυνίδιον ὡραῖον.
> <τὸ> κυνίδιον δ᾽ ἔχαιρε παῖζον εὐρύθμως,
> τὸν δεσπότην τε ποικίλως περισκαῖρον·
> κἀκεῖνος <αὖ> κατεῖχεν αὐτὸ τοῖς κόλποις.
> 5 ὁ δ᾽ ὄνος γ᾽ <ἔκαμνε> νύχθ᾽ <ὅλην> ἀλετρεύων
> πυρὸν φίλης Δήμητρος, ἡμέρης δ᾽ ὕλην
> κατῆγ᾽ ἀφ᾽ ὕψους, ἐξ ἀγροῦ θ᾽ ὅσων χρείη·

καὶ μὴν ἐν αὐλῇ παρὰ φάτναισι δεσμώτης
ἔτρωγε κριθὰς χόρτον, ὥσπερ εἰώθει.
10 δηχθεὶς δὲ θυμῷ καὶ περισσὸν οἰμώξας,
σκύμνον θεωρῶν ἁβρότητι σὺν πάσῃ,
φάτνης ὀνείης δεσμὰ καὶ κάλους ῥήξας
ἐς μέσσον αὐλῆς ἦλθ᾽ ἄμετρα λακτίζων.
σαίνων δ᾽ ὁποῖα καὶ θέλων περισκαίρειν,
15 τὴν μὲν τράπεζαν ἔθλασ᾽ ἐς μέσον βάλλων,
ἅπαντα δ᾽ εὐθὺς ἠλόησε τὰ σκεύη·
δειπνοῦντα δ᾽ ἰθὺς ἦλθε δεσπότην κύσσων,
νώτοις ἐπεμβάς· ἐσχάτου δὲ κινδύνου
θεράποντες ἐν μέσοισιν † ὡς εἶδον †
20 ἐσάωσαν < – × – ∪ – ∪ – – – >
κρανέης δὲ κορύναις ἄλλος ἄλλοθεν κρούων
ἔθεινον, ὥστε καὐτὸς ὕστατ᾽ ἐκπνείων
ʼἔτλην᾽ ἔλεξεν ʼοἶα χρή με, δυσδαίμων·
τί γὰρ παρ᾽ οὐρήεσσιν οὐκ ἐπωλεύμην,
25 βαιῷ δ᾽ ὁ μέλεος κυνιδίῳ παρισούμην;᾽

A man kept a donkey and a handsome little dog. The dog liked to play, leaping gracefully about his master in many artful ways; and the master in turn would hold him in his lap. The donkey in the evening toiled at grinding wheat, Demeter's gift, but in the daytime from the hills he hauled down wood, and from the fields such stuff as might be needed. Even in the courtyard he was tied a prisoner at the manger, where he munched his barley feed as usual day after day. Once, stung at the heart and groaning more than usual at his lot, seeing the puppy in the midst of every luxury, he broke the ropes that held him fastened to the donkey manger and sallied forth into the yard, kicking up his heels in awkward fashion. He sought to fawn upon his master and to jump around the way the dog would do. He burst into the dining room, where he broke the table and soon smashed all the furniture. Then he made for his master, who was eating his meal, and, intending to kiss him, he started to climb on his back. When the servants saw that their master was in great danger they managed to save him < . . . >. With hardwood clubs they set upon the donkey from all sides, beating him and pounding him unmercifully. Then said he, as he breathed his last, "I've suffered what I deserved, unlucky cuss. Why didn't I keep my station with the mules, instead of matching myself, to my ruin, with a little dog?"

In this text too one can, if one will, distinguish between an exposition, a central, and a final section (1–9, 10–18a, 18b–25). There is, however, neither any recognizable symmetry of the kind we find, for example, in the fable by Phaedrus which we looked at above, nor are there any clear markers for such structural divisions, such as we can observe in, again, Phaedrus's fable and in the Augustana text "The Donkey Who Would Be a Pet." On the contrary, Babrius's narration flows evenly as one organic unit. The poet achieves this by making the donkey the central figure throughout, unlike the author of the prose version, who features the dog in his exposition and the donkey in the main section, thereby contrasting the two. In Babrius the reader is taken through everything from the donkey's point of view: from the contrast between the two animals' situations—the ass's miserable existence is described more fully and, coming second, is given greater prominence—to the donkey's rampage from the manger onto its master's back, the clubs raining blows on it, and finally to its last words and final breath. This narrative stratagem makes the crucial difference, and in combination with Babrius's stylistic and metrical skills, which can only be accepted as a given in this brief introduction, ensures that readers will share the unfortunate beast's experiences and feelings.

Insight into the inner donkey is, then, the real theme in Babrius's version of this fable. M. Nøjgaard (1964–1967) was the first to observe—and rightly so—that here, and in several other of the poet's texts, the type of conflict that usually dominates in ancient fables, that is, between two characters, is recast as the inner conflict which one of the two fights out with its own self (2:206 ff.). Babrius's particular interest in the psychological motivation at play within a story means that he frequently modifies the genre's conventional narrative structure. He might, for example, condense or entirely omit the exposition or the concluding section (cf. Nøjgaard 218 ff. for such loci) or, alternatively, he might apportion to the summing-up given by one of the characters as much space within the poem as the rest of the text together (e.g., 63, 91), at times even more (51, 85). Little wonder that, in this author, a psychologizing approach to what goes on amongst the inhabitants of his fabulous world frequently outweighs, or even completely takes over, from the moralizing standpoint. The manuscripts do offer us an *epimythium* for every fable in Babrius, but meticulous textual analysis by the editors Luzzatto and La Penna has shown—and plausibly so—that in only 45 of the 144 fables in their Teubner edition can the lines which voice the *fabula docet* be regarded as genuine.

Babrius's fondness for psychologizing narration also means that he likes to insert dialogue into his fables (cf. esp. 50, 75, 92) and occasionally to switch to the epic mode. Homeric style is for him not just a means by which to parody epic poetry—his version of the war between the cats and mice (31) is a particularly good example of this—but quite clearly also an end in itself. He even goes so far as to render one fable, "The Stag Without a Heart" (95), in 102 verses and thus to make an *epyllion* of it. And Babrius displays not only a flair for 'epic,' but for 'epigram' too: one type of verse fable represented here eighteen times is the *tetrastichon*, which tells the story with epigrammatic succinctness in only four lines (not including the *epimythium*, that is) and ends on a witty note, reminiscent of many a quip in the *Anthologia Palatina* and in Martial (see *Mythiambi* 8, 14, 39, 40, 41, 54, 60, 73, 80, 81, 83, 90, 96, 109, 110, 113, 121, 133). Like most of Babrius's four-liners, the following example—fable 109—demonstrates that the poet will happily forego a chance to enlighten readers with a moral if he can offer them a bon mot instead:

> Μὴ λοξὰ βαίνειν᾽ ἔλεγε καρκίνῳ μήτηρ,
> ὑγρῇ τε πέτρῃ πλάγια κῶλα μὴ σύρειν.᾽
> ὁ δ᾽ εἶπε· ᾽μῆτηρ ἡ διδάσκαλος, πρώτη
> ὀρθὴν ἄπελθε, καὶ βλέπων σε ποιήσω.᾽

"Don't walk aslant!" said a mother crab to her young one. "Don't drag yourself crosswise over the wet rock." "Mother and teacher," replied the young crab, "first walk straight yourself, then I'll do so by watching you."

For the fable material in eleven of the eighteen *tetrasticha*, Babrius (or his 'epigones' Ps.-Dositheus, Aphthonius, and Avianus) is our only source, and so it seems reasonable to assume that he, like Phaedrus, not only created new versions of old tales, but also invented quite new ones. Of the 165 iambic fables that can definitely be attributed to Babrius (144 + frags. 1–21 Luzz.), a total of 72 could feasibly be his own original stories (cf. the *apparatus criticus* in Luzzatto and La Penna 1986). But where did he find the other 93 fables adapted in the *Mythiambi*? Did he use a fable book? And if so, which one?

Questions, questions, and even less chance of being able to answer them in Babrius's case than in Phaedrus's. We have no idea whether Babrius lived in the first century A.D.—he would then probably have used, as did Phaedrus, texts from a Hellenistic *repertorium*—or later, that is, in the second century, when his source could also have been a fable book from imperial times. Various indications suggest that the "King Alexander" to whose son Babrius addresses the prologue for book 2 (probably also that of book 1) is the Cilician *regulus* appointed, as we are told in Josephus's *Antiquitates Judaicae* 18.140, by Emperor Vespasian (69–79). However, the only really reliable date we have is provided by section 6 of Ps.-Dositheus's *Hermeneumata:* a note there tells us that this part of the schoolbook, the author of which knew the *Mythiambi,* was written in the year 207. Babrius must therefore have composed his fables before the beginning of the third century. Now, as we shall see below, "The Life and Fables of Aesop," the fable section of which was probably identical to the *Collectio Augustana,* was quite possibly written as early as the second century A.D. Babrius could, therefore, conceivably have taken his material from there. In fact, of the 93 fables in Babrius which are also to be found in other ancient authors and in his 'epigones,' 1 is also included in the *Aesop Romance,* and 78 appear in the *Collectio Augustana,* or at least in the Byzantine collections derived from this (cf. the *apparatus* in Perry 1965 to nos. 1–143, and in Luzzatto and La Penna 1986 to no. 144 and frags. 1–21).

There are, it must be noted, also motifs which appear in Babrius, in his 'epigones,' and otherwise only in Xenophon of Athens, Ennius, Horace, Phaedrus, Plutarch, and Gellius (cf. the critical apparatus in Luzzato and La Penna on 3, 24, 27–29, 33, 67, 78, 88, 100, 108, 128, 134, 142). Therefore, if Babrius did use the *Collectio Augustana,* he must have consulted earlier sources too. And since the anonymous author of the *Augustana* collection represents a fable tradition that reaches back into pre-Christian times, any correspondence between this writer and Babrius could be the result of both having read the same earlier sources. Again, the difficulties which arise when it comes to dating Babrius mean that anything we say about his possible sources must also remain open to question. Whatever the actual identity of Babrius's βασιλεὺς Ἀλέξανδρος, however, we may at least work on the assumption that the poet himself lived at the court of a minor ruler in the eastern half of the Roman Empire. He knows that the fable is a Babylonian "invention" (2. *prol*.1–3); he says that he has had personal experience of Arabs (57); and his vocabulary, as shown by M. J. Luzzatto (1975), includes diction similar to that of the Septuagint and the New Testament. The *regulus* whom Babrius served as court poet very probably ruled in Syria, a country where the author would find ample opportunities for collecting fable material from a variety of Greek and Near Eastern sources, written and oral.

King Alexander's son, who is addressed directly in the prologue to book 2, is probably identical with the "child" (τέκνον) Branchus, to whom Babrius turns in his prologue to book 1. Of the 45 *epimythia* in the *Mythiambi*, 17 are directed at a "you," including 2 cases where a vocative παῖ ("my son") is used, and one with the vocative Βράγχε (18.15; 72.23; 74.15). We may assume, then, that those of the poems which are at all moralizing in content were written for the benefit of the prince. The form of exhortation displayed in the 17 *epimythia* addressing a "you" makes these reminiscent of the "Thus you too . . ." endings which we find in the 'lone' fables used in varying literary and rhetorical contexts. By contrast, the conventional fable-book ending—"this fable shows . . ."—only appears six times in Babrius (22.13; 31.22; 36.13; 38.8; 56.8; 59.16; cf. 34.14; 40.5; 116.15; 119.11). The role of tutor adopted by the poet is underlined in 6 *epimythia* by the use of the first person (11.11; 14.5; 56.8; 57.12; 65.7; 66.7). And it can scarcely be pure coincidence that Babrius assigns the part of monitor or critic in four cases to an elderly animal (21, 24, 93, 104), especially as the extant parallel versions of two such fables include no corresponding finger-wagging figure (cf. 24 with Phaedrus 1.6, and 93 with *Ademar Codex* 43 = 63 Th. and *Aes*. 153).

Obviously the fabulous world which Babrius draws for his princely pupil—as we have already seen, it is a world defined in the prologue to book 1 as that of the "Golden Age"—is home to a firmly established monarchy. Whereas Phaedrus, in fables which involve the relations between ordinary people and those with power, betrays his own sympathies for the victims of despotism and violence, Babrius's attitude seems to tend toward the opposite. In some of his poems he quite definitely represents the antidemocratic viewpoint, most clearly so in fable 40. Here he tells the story—and his is our only version of this μῦθος—of a camel that relieves itself while crossing a river and sees its own dung being swept along in front of it by the current: "Truly, I'm in a bad way; what ought to be behind me is now going in front." The *epimythium* suggests that the fable can be applied to a city-state in which the lowest of citizens rule instead of the most noble. Babrius 134 (also in Plutarch, *Agis* 2) is similar in theme: a snake's tail rebels against the head, but all it accomplishes is that the whole snake promptly falls into a crevice and its spine takes a battering. The cartoon-like image of this inadvertent 'tail dive' makes the rebellion appear so ridiculous that one thing is immediately clear: Babrius has nothing but scorn for any uprising from the weaker end of the social hierarchy.

However emphatically this poet may plead for the supreme rule of the 'head' in a state, he also demands of kings that their regimes be well disposed toward their subjects. In order to express this with the help of fables he gives prominence, for example, to the above-mentioned group of tales about the lion by positioning them at the end of book 1. The king of beasts, moreover, possesses in some parts features characteristic of an ideal monarch. Fable 102, for instance—one which Babrius possibly created himself—tells how the animals would assemble under a lion's rule, this being a king "who had no cruel, brutish temper. He was not prone to settle things by force . . . but was of gentle mood and just, even as a man might be" (vv. 1–3). One of the kingly virtues named here, gentleness, is also expressly recommended by Babrius to King Alexander's son in the *epimythia* to fables 11 and 18; in 18.15–16, for example, he writes:

λέγει δ᾽ ὁ μῦθος· ᾽πραότητα, παῖ, ζήλου.
ἀνύσεις τι πειθοῖ μᾶλλον ἢ βίη ῥέζων.᾽

And the fable says: "Cultivate gentleness, my son; you will get results oftener by persuasion than by the use of force."

Both the ruling and the lower classes, then, are advised by Babrius to renounce violence. For the latter of these groups this means the ideology of conformity again, as propagated by Phaedrus. But whereas there, as we saw earlier, ordinary folk only accept their inevitable lot with much gnashing of teeth, here in Babrius they are ridiculed if they do not just grin and bear it. "The Fable's Revolt"? If there ever was such a thing in antiquity, then this poet was certainly not party to it.

* * *

Surveys of work on Babrius have only been compiled for a limited period—by Sitzler (1897–1922)—but there has in any case never been much to report. An extensive bibliography can be found on pages cxi–cxv of the excellent critical edition by Luzzatto and La Penna (1986), which has taken the place of Crusius (1897). No recent commentary exists, but Rutherford (1883) is still useful. The most important edition of the paraphrases remains that of the *Cod. Oxon. Bodleianus Auct. F. 4. 7* by Knöll (1877), as Chambry (1925) edited these texts together with those of the *Collectio Augustana* and its adaptations, making it rather difficult to identify any given fable text as a paraphrase of Babrius. Perry (1965) offers an English prose translation, and F. M. Garcia and A. R. Lopez provide an index (1990). The textual history of the fables has proved to be the main focus of research, and, in addition to Luzzatto and La Penna (1986, xxii ff.), the following must be named here: Hesseling (1892–1893), Crusius (1894), Ihm (1902), Radermacher (1902), Immisch (1930), Husselmann (1935), Vaio (1970, 1977, 1981, and 1984), and Adrados (1999b, 9–10). For general studies see Crusius (1879 and 1896b), Nøjgaard (1964–1967, 2:189–365, 2:432–438), Perry (1965, xlvii–lxxiii), Wagner (1977), Adrados (1979–1987, 2:173–212, and 2000, 175–220), and Luzzatto and La Penna (1986, vi–cxv); on Babrius's vita see Zimmermann (1933) and Vaio (1980); on style and metrics, see Luzzatto (1975 and 1985). The only existing reading through the eyes of literary criticism is found in Nøjgaard (supra), to which this introduction owes a great deal. There are, however, a few interpretations of individual fables available: on number 78, see Vaio (1994); on number 88, see Menna (1983), and on numbers 89 and 100, see Küppers (1990).

* * *

▮ Avianus, *Fabulae*

Anyone turning to the forty-two fables composed by Avianus around A.D. 400 will—especially anyone who comes directly from reading Phaedrus and Babrius—find it rather strange that this

Roman poet chose to write his Aesopica in, of all forms, a meter used for example by Ovid in his erotic poems: elegiac couplets. True, there was a certain 'tradition,' in Hellenistic and imperial Greek literature at least: in the *Anthologia Palatina* we find six epigrams which adapt fable motifs in elegiac couplets (6.217 = *Aes.* 436; 7.210 ~ *Aes.* 227; 9.3 ~ *Aes.* 250; 9.86 = *Aes.* 454; 9.99 ~ *Aes.* 374; 9.348 ~ *Aes.* 32). Even so, their authors were most probably not interested in the reader's moral edification, since none of the poems so much as hint at a *fabula docet*. These writers were obviously just enjoying the challenge of fitting material taken from the Aesopic narrative tradition into the structure of a typical epigram. The extant Greek and Roman fable books do contain many 'epigrammatically' constructed texts—the *tetrasticha* in Babrius, for example (supra, p. 58)—however, Avianus's fables are anything but short and pithy poems. His narrative technique is more reminiscent of Ovid's elegiac storytelling (e.g., in the *Fasti*), and the structure of the texts is not designed to have the reader laughing, or even merely smiling at the end, but rather concentrating entirely on the moral illustrated by the tale.

In the letter of dedication which precedes the fables, Avianus unfortunately offers no explanation as to why, when he makes "trees talk, wild beasts sigh together with humans, birds argue in words, and animals laugh," he does so in elegiac couplets. He does at least tell us why he chose the fable as such: because this genre allows the "untruth" (*falsitas*) as long as it is "elegantly couched" (*urbane concepta*), because it appeals to the fiction writer in him. Avianus goes on to present a brief survey of the genre's development from Aesop to Socrates and Horace—the last two representing those writers who use fables as exempla—and on to Babrius and Phaedrus. His aim here is apparently to imply that the fable can, in terms of literary history, claim respectability as a category. But what does he mean when, after this historical sketch, he says that he has assembled in one book 42 fables *quas rudi Latinitate compositas elegis sum explicare conatus*?

This much-debated relative clause can be read in two ways:

1. [Fables] "which I <, finding them to have been> written in plain Latin style <in the source I was using,> have tried to render in the elegiac meter," or

2. [Fables] "which I composed in plain Latin style, <but> have tried to render in the elegiac meter."

Those who prefer the first translation—that is, the majority of scholars since the days of Crusius (1896a)—understand the poet to have changed texts which he found in a collection of Latin fables from prose to verse. These texts would have to have been adaptations of poems by Babrius, since 35 of Avianus's tales are evidently somehow related either to fables in the *Mythiambi* manuscripts or to fables now identified as prose paraphrases of poems in Babrius; the remaining 7 fables in Avianus are probably based on now-lost poems from the *Mythiambi* (cf. the concordances in Küppers 1977, 164 and Luzzatto and La Penna 1986, xix–xxii). And—lo and behold!—Ausonius (ca. 310–395) makes a remark in one of his letters (16.2.74–81) from which one could, if one really must, infer that a certain Titianus did indeed turn fables by Babrius into Latin prose, and that these adaptations were later used by Avianus.

But is this really a 'must'? If one is not prepared to regard any deviations in Avianus from the corresponding fable in Babrius as part of the Latin author's own conception, well, yes, one must, because the Latin prose paraphrases of *Mythiambi* texts are then simply indispensable—where else could the changes in wording between Babrius and Avianus have surfaced? And because one can then conveniently ignore the possibility that the "Aesop in trimeters" which Ausonius's Titianus converted into prose could just as easily have been Phaedrus's *Fabulae Aesopiae* (even if this is the more obvious assumption, given that the paraphraser was writing in Latin). There is, however, an alternative. In his groundbreaking book on Avianus, J. Küppers meticulously analyses the differences between Avianus's fables and their counterparts in Babrius, and he concludes that there is a consistent underlying intention discernible throughout the Latin text. This intention is, furthermore, one that can only be explained on the basis of certain characteristic features of Avianus's treatment of fable motifs, of the Latin language, and of the elegiac meter. In the light of Küppers's arguments, we 'must' now tend instead toward the second translation: Avianus, whose praise of his dedicatee, Theodosius, as consummate rhetor and poet borders on the fulsome, is presenting himself for the rhetorical purposes of *captatio bene-volentiae* as a writer of lesser literary skill.

There is, then, no reason for us not to compare Avianus directly with Babrius, whose *duo volumina* are even mentioned in the Roman author's letter of dedication. Let us first consider this relationship in terms of book structure. Our premise here will be that the arrangement of Babrius's fables in the *Codex Athous* represents the original sequence in each book (see above, pp. 54–55). The order in which Avianus presents the fables borrowed from Babrius differs entirely from their order of appearance in the Greek text, and this we may take to be the result of deliberate planning. In the one currently available study on the structure of Avianus's *Fabulae*, M. J. Luzzatto (1984, 92–94) contends that 21 pairs of poems each link together comparable human failings or flaws, all exemplified by a fable. If we are willing to accept this theory—and not all instances in which Luzzatto would have us see a thematic connection are genuinely convincing—we must still reckon with the underlying presence of other structural principles within the two books. Fables 17 and 18 may well share the idea that "il pericolo non è sempre dove te lo aspetti" ("danger is not always where you expect it to be"), but the poem preceding number 17—"The Oak and the Reed"—manifestly has more to do with "The Pine and the Bramble Bush," which follows number 18, than with fable 15, "The Crane and the Peacock." Moreover, Avianus's opening *epistula* allows the assumption that the poet was familiar with Phaedrus's five books of *Fabulae Aesopiae*, and Küppers (1977, 142ff.) has even uncovered evidence which proves that Avianus, in two of his fables (34 and 37), uses thematically similar texts from Phaedrus (4.25 and 3.7). We must therefore also consider the possibility that Avianus's book composition could somehow be modeled on Phaedrus. Not here though—this is a subject for specialized study.

It is time now for an example of how Avianus structures his fables and forms them in terms of style and meter. We shall look at "The Crab and Its Mother" (3: text based on Duff and Duff 1934), which we saw earlier in the version by Babrius (supra, p. 58).

> *Curva retro cedens dum fert vestigia cancer,*
> *hispida saxosis terga relisit aquis.*

hunc genetrix facili cupiens procedere gressu
   talibus alloquiis emonuisse datur:
5   'ne *tibi transverso placeant haec devia, nate*
   rursus in obliquos neu velis ire pedes,
sed nisu contenta ferens vestigia recto
   innocuos proso tramite siste gradus.'
cui natus "faciam, si me praecesseris" inquit
10   'rectaque *monstrantem certior ipse sequar.*
nam stultum nimis est, cum tu pravissimia temptes,
   alterius censor si vitiosa notes.'

While a crab was walking backwards and tracing its crooked way, it banged its scaly back in the rocky pools. Its mother, eager to go forward with step unhindered, is said to have delivered a warning to it in such words as these: "Don't go zigzag and choose these crooked ways, my child, and don't seek to move backwards and slantwise on your feet. Step out vigorously with straightforward effort and plant your footsteps safely in the onward path." "I will do so," the young crab replied, "if you go ahead of me; and, if you show me the correct road, I will follow the more surely. For it is exceedingly foolish of you, when you are attempting the most crooked of courses yourself, to set up as censor and criticize the faults of another."

The four *choliambi* in Babrius have been turned into six elegiac distichs by Avianus. Whereas the Greek fabulist concentrates on the actual story, that is, the dialogue between the two crustaceans, the Roman poet adds an exposition, introducing the crab mother in one couplet, the son in another; admonition and retort then take up two couplets respectively, as opposed to the one-and-a-half *choliambi* each are given in Babrius.

How this choice of meter affects the actual telling of a fable is immediately clear. As in the elegiac narratives of, for example, Ovid, where the pentameter often repeats in only slightly modified form what has been said in the hexameter, the couplets 5–6, 7–8, and 9–10 here reiterate as well. The juxtaposition of hexameter and pentameter also lends itself to the creation of antitheses, and Avianus too makes use of this—here for maximum effect in the final couplet, which articulates the fable's moralizing core: "do not demand of others what you cannot do yourself." Only in the four opening verses does each line represent one statement, and the last of these in any case only tells us—with epic fullness—that someone then said something to someone else.

What does Avianus achieve by rendering the fable in this form? First, the narrative becomes wholly subordinate to the *fabula docet* it is illustrating, because it is split up into a veritable chain of antitheses. The crablet's funny walk is contrasted with the way his mother wants him to walk (1–3). The two lines in which the mother tells the son what he is not to do (5–6) are followed by two in which she tells him what he should do (7–8), with the hexameter here creating an additional antithesis to the poem's opening line (1: *retro . . . fert vestigia;* 7: *[nisu] . . . ferens vestigia recto*). The penultimate couplet, in which the crablet says how he expects his "teacher" to bear herself, is contrasted with the final one (assumed here to be genuine), where the mother's actual deportment is characterized, with yet another antithesis there in the shape of *tu . . . alterius*.

The narrative articulation of these antithesis-packed contents, for which Babrius, in his epigram-style fable, takes two iambic couplets, is stretched by Avianus to cover six couplets in dactylic verse, making it three times as long. The plot of the fable, which could scarcely be simpler, is thus spun out as far as it will go (but at the expense of the Babrius's original quip). At the same time, however—and this is the second effect achieved through Avianus's chosen form of adaptation—the rhetorical elaboration of an uncomplicated story gives the author an opportunity to display all his skills in the art of poetic embellishment. He dazzles here with ample sprinklings of the diction traditionally used in elegiac narrative, elsewhere with phrases coined to echo Virgil and introduced solely for stylistic effect (cf. the allusions identified by Küppers 1977, 107–108, 139–140, 151–152).

Predictably, this joining of rhetoric and poetry, which is typical of Avianus's entire fable book, has frequently incurred the scorn of critics. "The young man's work cannot be called well executed" is the verdict of Schanz, Hosius, and Krüger, not—as one might be forgiven for thinking—in an end-of-term report, but in their history of Roman literature (4.2, Munich 1920, 33). "He is mostly long-winded and boring," Hausrath finds (1983, 1494). And even Küppers (1977), who produced the first profound analysis of

Avianus's fables and in it the first accurate picture of this poet's methods, cannot resist numbering the texts "amongst the less outstanding and more insignificant items in Rome's literary bequest" (68) and rounding off his very constructive book with the assessment: "All in all, Avianus proves to be a mediocre poet" (235).

Scholars working on Avianus—and indeed not a few classicists interpreting other authors—tend to let themselves be guided by a vision of what the text in hand should ideally look like, thereby neglecting the real task of literary criticism: to bring to light by objective scrutiny the author's reasons for writing what he did the way he did, and to consider how far his intention was determined by the age in which he lived. In Avianus's case the answers are clearly the following: he decides to write a fable book and finds himself faced with a number of illustrious predecessors in the genre; he plans to outshine them all by trying to make his poems fulfill even more proficiently the requirement this literary form is expected to meet. What must he do? He must ensure that his fables combine fictional narrative with moral edification (see above, p. 20). And so Avianus crosses rhetorical debate, which weighs the pros and cons of an ethical problem, with elegiac narrative, the preferred model for grooming his poetic diction being the most prestigious writer of dactylic verse and prince of poets, Virgil.

As to the historical background against which Avianus's fables must be seen, we know little more than what he himself tells us in the *epistula* to a Theodosius. Even the identification of the addressee is subject to controversy. The majority of scholars believe him to be Macrobius Ambrosius Theodosius, who lived around A.D. 400 and wrote the dialogue *Saturnalia*, as well as a commentary on Cicero's *Somnium Scipionis*; some even claim that the historical figure behind the Avienus in said *Saturnalia* must therefore be our Avianus. Küppers (1977) advances good reasons for not linking the poet with this work (28 ff.), but still believes that Macrobius must be the Theodosius in the *epistula*. His argumentation is based primarily on an illustration of this letter found in the *Cod. Paris. Lat. (nouv. acq.)* 1132, which shows Avianus handing his fable book to its dedicatee; Küppers thinks that both persons in this drawing can be identified as men of letters. M. J. Luzzatto (1984, 89–91), on the other hand, believes the figure accepting the fables to be someone of high rank, and so agrees with those scholars who identify the *epistula*'s Theodosius as one of the two Roman emperors that bear this name. Her personal vote goes to Theodosius II (A.D. 408–450), who, as Luzzatto rightly stresses, actively supported the scholarly and literary activities of both Greek and Latin-speaking rhetors, being himself a "uomo colto e καλλίγραφος"; one impressive manifestation of this is the university in Constantinople which he founded in the year A.D. 425.

The identity of the letter's Theodosius remaining uncertain, attempts like those of Küppers's (1977) to investigate the poet's 'literary habitat'—and thus track down any topical allusions his work may contain—are of dubious value. Both the *epistula* and the fables themselves make it in any case quite clear that Avianus did not choose this genre because he thought it would enable him to express his views on current political, social, or ethical problems. Nor is there so much as a trace here of Phaedrian social satire or Babrian reflections on a monarch's rights and obligations. Avianus's observation as to the beneficial effects reading his fables will have on their addressee are nothing but conventional topoi: *habes ergo opus, quo animum oblectes, ingenium exerceas, sollicitudinem leves totumque vivendi ordinem cautus agnoscas* ("You have, therefore, a work to delight the mind, to exercise the brain, to relieve anxiety—one that will give you a wary knowledge of the whole course of life").

Avianus apparently decided to write verse fables simply because he was hoping for the recognition and appreciation a particular literary circle might then offer him—a circle in which his Theodosius played a leading role and which had so far not cultivated this genre. And it was not the opportunity afforded by the fable for the articulation of ideological sentiments that attracted him. No, it was the chance to prove his virtuosity and formal artistry as a poet under the challenging circumstances which, in Avianus's eyes, this kind of text presented: the use of fiction as basis for a display of narrative skill, the renown enjoyed by previous fabulists—these virtually asking to be imitated, even outdone—and the narrative material's suitability for adaptation in verse. This last consideration will have been an added encouragement to create, by using a meter hitherto not associated with the genre, a type of fable that was—in terms of form at least—quite new.

The results of this venture were to become so popular in the Middle Ages that Avianus's fables were spared the fate suffered by those of Phaedrus and Babrius. The *Fabulae Aesopiae* and *Mythiambi* sank for the most part into oblivion because there were prose paraphrases available. Avianus's elegiac tales may not have escaped rehashing either, but the original texts continued to be copied, and over one hundred such codices written between the ninth and sixteenth centuries survive (cf. Guaglianone 1958, ix–xxviii). Of course, today's classicists may, if they so wish, interpret this very popularity—especially Avianus's inclusion in medieval school curricula—as confirmation of their own negative assessment of the fables' literary qualities. And yet it must be remembered that Ovid, now recognized as one of antiquity's most fascinating 'giants' (even if it has taken a while for such recognition to become global), was so avidly read by twelfth-century 'dwarves' that this period is known as the *aetas Ovidiana*. Perhaps those who pronounce Avianus lacking as a poet should reconsider their verdict.

* * *

As in work on Phaedrus, new studies on Avianus's fables were listed regularly before the Second World War (Draheim 1889–1925, Port 1933–1939), but not afterward. Editions of the poems are to be found in Ellis (1887; includes the only existing commentary on the fable book), in Duff and Duff (1934; with an English prose translation), in Guaglianone (1958), and in Gaide (1980; with a French translation). For an index see de Paulis (1997). The textual history is discussed by Jones (1940) and Guaglianone (1956 and 1957). Of the few general works published, the following make useful reading: Crusius (1896a), Adrados (1979–1987, 2:243–260, and 2000, 254–274). Küppers (1977) is a monograph which merits particular mention because it provides the first interpretation of the fables; it is best read in conjunction with the article by Luzzatto (1984), this offering a critical discussion of Küppers with important additional ideas (e.g., on the analysis of the book structure). Some specialized studies—on the vita and on the question of sources—published before Küppers's book are still valuable: Unrein (1885), Cameron (1967), Thraede (1968–1969), and Jones (1969). Gaide (1991) also attempts a macroscopic reading, but declares Avianus in the end "mediocre" (as did Küppers

1977, 255); one must continue to wonder, then, why, in the Middle Ages, this poet was "one of the most-read authors of western Christendom" (Wright 1997, 10). For discussions of specific fables, see Pillolla (1991) on 14 and 20; Menna (1983) on 21; and Küppers (1990) on 37.

3

Fable Books in Prose

■ **"The Life and Fables of Aesop"**

There survive a large number of Greek manuscripts from the tenth to the sixteenth centuries which contain prose fables ascribed to Aesop, and in many of these codices the tales are preceded by a fictional biography of the "author": the *Vita Aesopi,* or *Aesop Romance.* Neither the text of the vita nor that of the fables exists in one universal *recensio,* so that we have, in all, three different traditions for the life and, excluding those of the fables which paraphrase poems by Babrius (supra, p. 53), three again for the works. In each case—vita and fable corpus—one of these received versions can probably be traced back to antiquity, while the other two are later in origin. The textual history of the *Aesop Romance* and that of the Aesopica are strikingly similar, and the following question therefore arises: are all *recensiones* involved ultimately derived from one single book, the author of which presented it to readers as a sort of make-believe collected edition with an allegedly definitive biography—"The Life and Fables of Aesop"?

Let us first consider the relationship between the *Romance* manuscript traditions themselves and between the three traditions and their shared ancestor, the lost original vita. The contents and wording of this archetype are in all likelihood quite reliably represented by *Vita G,* which has come down to us in one codex only: formerly kept in Grottaferrata (hence the *G*), then untraceable for a while, it now forms *Codex 397* of the Pierpont Morgan Library in New York. *Vita W* (named after the *editio princeps* by Westermann 1845), on the other hand, is an epitome; the story is told there over long passages in condensed form, and several sections contained in *Vita G* are missing. However, *Vita W* is not an abridged version of *Vita G* because, for one thing, the five papyrus fragments of the *Aesop Romance* which have so far been unearthed (cf. Beschorner and Holzberg 1992, 165–168) offer some text that corresponds to G and some that corresponds to W; also, three episodes found in the W-tradition manuscripts (chapters 50a, 77a, 77b) are missing in *Vita G*. The third version of the *Aesop Romance* can be ascribed to the editorial hand of the Byzantine scholar Maximus Planudes (ca. 1255–1305); labeled *Vita Pl*, it comprises an adaptation of *Vita W*, but with no fundamental changes.

Planudes probably also edited one of the three fable collections, *recensio III*, or *recensio Accursiana*, after Bonus Accursius, who was responsible for its first publication around 1479. Of the 127 fables there, 62 are adapted from texts in *recensio II*, also known as the *recensio Vindobonensis* (after the *Codex Vindob. gr. hist. 130*); the others are almost all adaptations from *recensio I*, that is, the *recensio Augustana* (after *Codex Monacensis gr. 564*, originally kept in Augsburg), on which the *Vindobonensis* collection with its 130 fables was largely based. The *recensio Augustana*, then, represents the oldest of the three traditions. Its 231 fables (= *Aes.* 1–231), to which can perhaps be added 13 texts only found in what is known as *recensio Ia* (= *Aes.* 232–244), also make it the largest of the collections.

In the oldest extant "Aesop" manuscript, the tenth-century *Codex G*, the *Augustana* collection appears in conjunction with *Vita G*, the version of the *Aesop Romance* that is most closely related to the archetype. This is of considerable significance for the question of a possible ancient and now-lost "Life and Fables of Aesop." In the manuscript tradition, the joint transmission of the fables ascribed to Aesop and his fictional biography is not restricted to this one combination of *Vita G* and the *Augustana* collection in New York's *Codex G*. We also have the following examples (cited here with the sigla used by Perry 1952):

1. *Vita G* came before the *Collectio Augustana* in the copy text for *Codex Pa*, later to be replaced there with Ps.-Aphthonius's brief life of Aesop (= *Test.* 1 Perry), a text which reads less like a novel and more like reliable historical information; the last two sentences of *Vita G* were left standing, probably due to an oversight (cf. Perry 1936, 166–167.).

2. *Vita W* is linked in *Pg* with the *Collectio Augustana*, in *Cb, Cf, Ci, F, L*, and *M* with fables from *recensio II*, and in *Ca* with a collection which combines fables from both of these *recensiones*.

3. *Vita Pl* is, in those manuscripts which contain fables and this text, always preceded by the *Accursiana* collection.

Except in the manuscripts *Pg* and *Ca*, then, the vita *recensiones* always appear together with the corresponding *recensio* of the fables. This would seem to be a very persuasive argument in favor of the assumption that there was indeed an ancient "edition" of Aesop in which the Βίος Αἰσώπου was followed by the Αἰσώπου Μῦθοι. The theory is also supported by a sentence in chapter 100 of the *Aesop Romance:* "Aesop then wrote down for him [King Croesus] his own fables and stories, the ones that can still be read today, and left them with him for the library" (Αἴσωπος οὖν αὐτῷ συγγραψάμενος τοὺς ἰδίους λόγους καὶ μύθους, τοὺς ἄχρι καὶ νῦν ἀναγινωσκομένους, κατέλιπεν εἰς τὴν βιβλιοθήκην). Considering that, with the exception of the *Aesop Romance*, almost all ancient *testimonia* for Aesop only talk of a λογοποιός who presented his λόγοι καὶ μῦθοι orally, we might well ask whether the above-quoted assertion in the *Romance* is not a subtle attempt to lend the book's contents an authentic ring. Not only does it "prove" to readers that this particular episode in Aesop's life must have taken place, it also encourages them to believe that the collection following the "biography" is in fact the very body of fables ("that can still be read today") created by the famous storyteller portrayed in the vita, one who had not previously been known to have put his "creations" down in writing (something otherwise only mentioned in Aphthonius, *Progymnasmata* 1).

If these arguments are correct, the next question is this: does the fictitious authentication introduced by the vita's author, that is, the establishment of Aesop as author of the collection that follows, have any truth to it, at least insofar as the fables presented were not written by the author of the life, but by a different anonymous author? Or did the "biographer" write these as well? The approximate dating which the extant textual material suggests for the archetypes of the *Aesop Romance* and the *Collectio Augustana* certainly does not rule out the second possibility. One of the papyrus fragments of the vita, *P.Berol. inv. 11628,* can be assigned to the second or third century A.D., which places the original for the *Romance* in the first half of Rome's imperial age. And this, in turn, is the very era to which some scholars convincingly date the archetype of the *recensio Augustana.* The language of the fables in this collection is plain and unadorned, that is, largely lacking in rhetorical embellishment, and is reminiscent on the one hand of the fable *repertorium* fragmentarily preserved *Papyrus Rylands 493,* and on the other, at least in some places, of Phaedrus's mode of expression. Even if the author of the *Collectio Augustana* is, as we shall see later, likely to have chosen simple diction deliberately, this stylistic similarity between the fables there and in the two first-century collections makes a composition date in the earlier rather than the later years of the empire seem more plausible.

There is, however, one strong argument against the theory that the original vita and *Collectio Augustana* were written by the same author. Five fables occur both in the one and in the other—the *Romance* shows Aesop telling four of these λόγοι, each in a specific, relevant situation (chap. 48 ~ *Aes.* 85; chap. 97 ~ *Aes.* 153; chap. 125 ~ *Aes.* 177; chaps. 135–139 ~ *Aes.* 3), and the fifth is used as the central motif in one episode of the novel's plot (chaps. 35–37 ~ *Aes.* 119)—but their outward form differs in the "biography" entirely from their appearance amongst the "collected fables." This observation suggests that, for the second part of his "edition," the author of the vita took a collection of Aesopica that was already in existence.

And yet the *Aesop Romance* and the *Collectio Augustana* do have one feature in common that permits us at least to wonder whether "The Life and Fables of Aesop" could have been the work of one single author after all. As M. Nøjgaard argued on very convincing grounds over thirty years ago (1:131 ff.), the *Collectio Augustana* was conceived as one homogeneous narrative unit, and very recent studies on the *Aesop Romance* demonstrate that this text too follows a specific and consistent structural pattern (infra, pp. 79 ff.). Could it not have been the same author in both cases—one possessed of considerable compositional skills and thus able to create each part of the book in accordance with the relevant generic conventions, that is, with those conventions for novel-like biographies and those for fable books? Such an author might have made a conscious and deliberate distinction between fables presented orally by Aesop because of their relevance to a given situation, and fables which the λογοποιός put down in writing; this would explain why the stories told by the Aesop of the vita are different in form from their counterparts in the "edition." But without comparative analyses of the language and style used in the *Aesop Romance* and in the *Collectio Augustana*, we are, admittedly, on dangerously thin conjectural ice here.

"THE LIFE OF AESOP": THE *AESOP ROMANCE*

Although the *Aesop Romance* can be numbered alongside Petronius's *Satyrica* and the *Metamorphoses* of Apuleius as an ancient precursor of the modern picaresque novel, narratologists have only recently begun to take an interest in it; previous studies of the book were restricted to textual criticism and an approach colored by source-oriented historicism. The kind explanation for this curious state of affairs would be that the manuscript of *Vita G* was quite a late discovery, and that research on it was therefore still in its infancy. However, even *Vita G*'s first editor, B. E. Perry (1952)—just like earlier *Aesop Romance* scholars, who had only known the epitomized versions *W* and *Pl*—formed a very low opinion of the intellectual caliber and literary abilities of its author. The real reason why, until lately, no proper interpretations of the novel have been forthcoming is, then, simply (and less kindly) that no one thought it was worth it.

Lessing's philologist friend Johann Jakob Reiske once dismissed the *Aesop Romance* as "unfunny Greek Eulenspiegel pranks" and as "pitiful entertainment for the common herd" (cf. Foerster 1895), and verdicts remained similarly crushing in literature on the text for a long time. They culminated in the following remark by Antonio La Penna: "anche i più fanatici credenti nella potenza ingenua dell'arte popolare si sentirebbero imbarazzati di fronte a questa Vita" (1962, 313: "even the most fanatical of believers in the naïve appeal of popular literature would be disconcerted in the face of this vita"). One very common reason for such damning appraisal was that the *Aesop Romance* was found lacking in any underlying pattern or structure. La Penna concluded that it was safe "to remove and insert at will" the different parts of the novel "without detriment to the rest," as is typical of "works that are not organic corpora, whole in themselves" (ibid.). To B. Holbek, each section of the vita seems to have "its own individual character," and so "the linking of all the parts to form one comprehensive narrative . . . has not been all that successful" (1977, 886).

No explicit evidence is ever offered for findings of this nature, but the basis for the verdict "clumsy patchwork" is not hard to trace: it lies in the one-sided analytical method that focuses solely on a text's possible sources. Until a short time ago, the *Aesop Romance* was thought to be the result of an unknown author's efforts to compile a fictional vita from an existing stock of textual material. Before we take a look at how the anonymous is generally supposed to have stitched the pieces together, a brief sketch of their contents is in order.

The story opens with the Phrygian slave Aesop, from birth a mute, being given the ability to speak by the goddess Isis as reward for a pious deed; in addition, the Muses endow him with particular eloquence. Later he comes to live on the island of Samos as a slave of the philosopher Xanthus, on whom he plays a number of crude practical jokes; after helping his master out of three tricky situations and correctly interpreting an eagle's portentous behavior for the Samians, he is made a freedman. The *prodigium* had been a warning that King Croesus would conquer Samos, but Aesop is able to prevent this by gaining the Lydian's favor with a fable. The hero then goes off to Babylon, helps King Lycorus solve some brain-teasing riddles of the type which Near Eastern rulers liked to pose to one another, and thereby secures for the Babylonian monarch high tribute payments from King Nectanebo of Egypt. There follows a trip through Greece, with Aesop giving various brilliant demonstrations of his talent as λογοποιός, not unlike the itinerant rhetors of the first/second centuries A.D. The people of Delphi feel insulted by a fable he tells there, so the priests of Apollo smuggle a golden bowl from the temple into his luggage and then sentence him to death for stealing it. Aesop tries to put the fear of the gods into them with suitable fables, but, undaunted, they take him to the top of a cliff; he forestalls the execution by jumping to his death. The gods duly visit their wrath upon the Delphians by sending a plague; an oracle tells them that they must pay for Aesop's untimely end, and later the Greeks, Babylonians, and Samians wreak military vengeance.

Until very recently, studies published on the *Aesop Romance* wanted us to believe that the sections before and after Aesop's adventures in the Near East were borrowed more or less as a whole from an existing text. German scholars once imagined this source to be a prose folk book dating from the fifth century B.C. or even earlier. Another, later theory suggested that the author had various anecdotes about Aesop at his disposal—some written, some from oral tradition—which, requiring virtually no changes, only needed to be strung together loosely. Between the two narrative blocks created in this way (chaps. 1–100, set for the most part on Samos, and 124–142, set mainly in Delphi) the anonymous author then, so the argument goes, clumsily inserted the account of Aesop's exploits in Babylon and Egypt (chaps. 101–123). These had originally been the exploits of a wise Assyrian vizier, Ahikar, which our anonymous had found in a Greek translation of the *Ahikar Romance* (see above, pp. 14–15) and of course borrowed, substituting Aesop for the original hero. What, one might ask, would have been the point of such a crude cut-and-paste job? The answer commonly given was put as follows in a handbook on the ancient novel, written by someone whose name may be familiar: "in order to create a framework for a collection of Aesopic fables" (Holzberg, *Der antike Roman*, Munich and Zurich 1986, 23).

The insufficient data that backed this statement has since been supplemented by a more thorough analysis of the *Aesop Romance*, so that this 'capital mistake' must be revised here. The following two theories can now be seen to hold:

1. Regarding the anonymous author's handling of source material: the original version of the *Aesop Romance*—written in the imperial age—did not simply comprise a string of loosely connected episodes, but was conceived as a homogenous narrative unit. Its author was inspired in no small measure by the

Ahikar Romance, and in fact most of the *facta* and *dicta* attributed here to the fabulist are drawn from other lives; the subjects of these were great minds comparable to Aesop—Hesiod, the "Seven Sages," Socrates, and Diogenes of Sinope, to name the most frequently used instances. Relatively little material, by contrast, was adopted from the existing biographical tradition for Aesop. Our anonymous author, we may therefore conclude, did not just take his pick from the available stock and merely adapt this compilation to suit prevalent tastes. Rather, he transposed the motifs he had borrowed, thus forming new episodes which he then assembled according to a carefully devised plan. The result: a new literary work.

2. Regarding the relationship between the plot of the novel and the inserted λόγοι (why this more general label is used here rather than the term *fable* will become clear presently): Aesopic λόγοι were not slotted into the account primarily for the sake of telling them. They were deliberately selected and employed by the author because their form and content would suggest the interpretation to be read into the given "biographical" context.

The structural analysis which formed the basis for these two contentions yielded a number of observations, and the following is a summary of the findings.

Whereas previous studies on the *Aesop Romance* tended to divide the text into the three parts "Aesop on Samos," "Aesop in the Near East," and "Aesop in Delphi," the novel's contents can now be seen to fall into five sections: 1. Prelude (chaps. 1–19); 2. Aesop and Xanthus (chaps. 20–91), with the three subdivisions— 2a. Aesop joins Xanthus's household as slave (20–33), 2b. Aesop plays practical jokes on his master (34–64), and 2c. Aesop helps his master (65–91)—3. Aesop helps the Samians (chaps. 92–100); 4. Aesop helps King Lycorus of Babylon (chaps. 101–123); and 5. Aesop in Delphi, unable to help himself (chaps. 124–142).

This framework is supported by various structural devices, the most important of which are two principles of composition:

1. strategic variation between the three kinds of Aesopic λόγοι used in the novel;
2. the construction of three-stage action sequences.

The first principle involves the deployment of the following
λόγος types:

A. direct precepts (monologue, dialogue);
B. solutions to a problem (difficult task, question, riddle);
C. fables of specific relevance to a given situation.

These are not simply chosen at random—the author inserts
them in strategic fashion over the course of the novel's five sections. Thus

1. in the prelude (1) Aesop does not say much—in chapters 1–7
   he is still mute—and only sets about offering someone his precepts three times;
2. in section 2, where Aesop is Xanthus's slave, and in section 4,
   which is set in the Near East, type A (direct precepts) and type
   B (problem solutions) are used; in section 2 only type A appears
   in modified form, showing Aesop—like the roguish hero of
   the German *Till Eulenspiegel* tales—taking his master's orders
   too literally and thereby teaching him a lesson;
3. in section 3, where Aesop helps the Samians against King
   Croesus, and section 5, which is set in Delphi, only fables with
   specific relevance to the events are used; in the Samian section
   they always achieve the desired effect, but in the Delphian,
   never.

Their distribution in tabular form:

```
       1  Aesop mostly silent
   ⌐   2  λόγος type A and B
   |   3  λόγος type C (effect as desired)      ⌐
   └   4  λόγος type A and B                    |
       5  λόγος type C (effect not as desired)  ⌐
```

Even this simple schematic representation shows us again how
securely the adaptation of the *Ahikar Romance* (4) is woven into
the overall plot of this novel; for one, it is coupled thematically to
section 2, and then it is encased by the 'frames-for-fables' sections 3 and 5. Furthermore, the chain of events in Babylon and
Egypt is strikingly similar to the scenario for section 3: in both a

king's letter sets things in motion (chaps. 92 and 105); in both Aesop undertakes a long journey in order to solve the problem caused by the arrival of a letter (chaps. 98 and 111); and in both a λόγος triptych is inserted into the plot, in section 3 as fables applicable to the current predicament (chaps. 94, 97, 99), and in section 4 as answers to riddles (chaps. 117–122). Significantly, none of the events reported in section 3 are mentioned in older narrative material on the life of Aesop; this merely tells us that he was once consulted by the people of Samos and that he once stayed at the court of Croesus (*Test.* 33–38 and 41 Perry). It seems safe to assume, then, that the Greek version of the *Ahikar Romance,* which is supposed to have been wedged clumsily into the *Vita Aesopi,* in fact furnished the latter's author with structural and thematic ideas for the conception of section 3.

On now to the second principle of composition: the construction of three-stage action sequences. Let us see how the author achieves this within one of the five main divisions in his work. Our example, section 2: Aesop and Xanthus, is divided into an exposition (chaps. 20–33) and two blocks of episodes; the first of these, chapters 34–64, is characterized by λόγοι of the "direct precept by taking an order too literally" kind, while the second, chaps. 65–91, is characterized by the "solution to a problem" type. In both cases the λόγος forms the central part in each of three lengthier episodes. First to the (modified) type A λόγος: Aesop prepares one single lentil (φακός) as dinner for Xanthus and all his guests, his master having ordered him to cook φακός, albeit in the collective singular sense of "lentil dish" (chaps. 39–43). The second episode centers around Aesop's personal interpretation of an order telling him to serve the leftovers from a dinner party to a female who is fondly disposed to his master: the slave gives them not to Xanthus's wife, but to his female dog (chaps. 44–50). The central element in the third episode is Aesop's repeated serving of pig's tongue in reaction to two orders, the first being to prepare that which is most useful in life, the second, to prepare that which is most detrimental (chaps. 51–64).

Now we will consider type B. The Xanthus section closes with a second block of episodes in which Aesop thrice helps his master to solve a problem. In chapters 68–74 a student asks Xanthus whether a man could drink the ocean dry, and the philosopher boasts that he personally could; he only wins the ensuing bet because Aesop advises him to request that all river mouths be blocked off before he starts drinking. In chapters 78–80 Xanthus is unable to decipher the inscription on a tombstone, but Aesop can and promptly finds some buried treasure, which ends up in his master's possession. In chapters 81–91 Xanthus is asked by the Samians to interpret an eagle's ominous behavior, but he is unable to do so and decides to kill himself; Aesop comes to the rescue with the correct explanation. Taken as a linear sequence, the endings of the three episodes here create a sort of climactic buildup. In chapter 74 Aesop asks to be set free as reward for helping his master, but his request is denied. In chapter 80 Xanthus, who had actually promised Aesop his freedom, has him tied up instead. And in chapter 90 the slave's wish is finally granted.

So much, then, for our examples of three-stage sequences. The motif mentioned briefly there—"Aesop's undeserved imprisonment"—brings us to one of several thematic strands, each of which forms a connection between the different sections of the novel, and each of which is woven in three phases. Aesop is unjustly incarcerated three times in all. Xanthus has him wrongfully tied up (chap. 80); when he is slandered and the king of Babylon condemns him to death, he is kept hidden in a prison (chap. 104); and, finally, the Delphians throw Aesop into jail for a crime he did not commit (chap. 128). In the first two cases he is set free because the person responsible for his imprisonment wants him to solve a problem, but in the third he is taken directly from the prison to the place of execution. This threesome finds a parallel in the three appearances of the motif "wrongfully accused of theft." In the exposition Aesop is unjustly accused of stealing figs (chap. 3). In the Xanthus section the philosopher removes one of the pig's trotters being cooked for a dinner party from the pot so that Aesop will get into trouble (chap. 42). And in the last section of the novel an innocent Aesop is charged with stealing from the temple (chap. 128). Again he is twice able to extricate himself, and again on the third occasion he fails.

He fails, moreover, even although he tells the Delphians taking him to the execution site four fables which he thinks will bring home to them the shamefulness of their present actions (chaps. 132–141). At the beginning of the novel, by comparison,

Aesop manages to clear himself of the wrongful charge, although he is still a mute and has to conduct his defense with sign language and gesticulations (chap. 3). The opening and closing sections of the book thus form a contrast that is deliberate and is clearly meant to tell us something: as slave and mute Aesop is able to keep his enemies at bay, but as a rich and famous itinerant speaker he seeks in vain to save his skin with his λόγοι. This is so blatantly paradoxical that it must surely be the narrator's way of expressing his view of the behavior displayed by Aesop after the gods have endowed him with λογοποιία.

The explanation for this radical inversion of the fabulist's earlier experiences lies in the three-stage development of the plot in the central part of the novel, that is, in sections 2, 3, and 4. There Aesop appears first as a 'troubleshooter' for Xanthus, next for the Samians, and then for King Lycorus, the recipients of his help coming in each instance from progressively higher rungs on the social ladder. This three-stage sequence is combined with a development in Aesop's character from piousness—by which he distinguishes himself particularly in the exposition—to increasingly manifest hubris, with which he eventually brings the wrath of Apollo upon himself. Right after his first big success at solving problems—his mediation between the Samians and King Croesus—he makes his first big mistake. In the temple which he dedicates to the Muses in appreciation of their gift, the statue he has raised in their midst is not one of Apollo Musagetes, but of himself (chap. 100.12–14 [Papathomopoulos 1991]); later he makes things even worse by insulting the inhabitants of Delphi, the sacred city. Apollo subsequently supports his priests in their conspiracy against Aesop and thus plays a part in the fabulist's death.

Aesop's rise and fall is very reminiscent of the fate suffered by many a tragic hero, such as Oedipus, for example: he helps the people of Thebes by solving a riddle and is made king, but he fails to interpret correctly the Delphian oracle regarding his own person and so comes to grief. The author of the *Aesop Romance* clearly wanted to present his hero as the type of sage who is first superior to all in his surroundings, but ends up blinded by this very superiority. One further intention is also clear, however, which was doubtlessly equally important in the author's mind: the unmasking of discrepancies between appearance and reality in the behavior displayed by some of the characters Aesop encounters. Narrative motifs such as "mute exposes talking persons" and "born a slave but smarter than a philosopher, a council and people's assembly of an entire state, and mighty kings together" would fit very nicely into any of the genres which portray a "topsy-turvy world," and especially into social and moral satire.

How deeply committed the anonymous author of the *Aesop Romance* was to the kind of issues satire might focus on is something that only analyses which look at the text's possible message and topicality within its historical context can tell us. No such studies exist at present, and the approach would be a difficult one, since we know absolutely nothing about the author and can only put a very approximate date to the book. This much we can say: it is not only the skill on which we have focused above, that is, the ability to combine the hero's adventures and make of them integral parts of a narrative whole, that links this Greek author with the writers of picaresque novels—the view of the world and its inhabitants presented here does so too.

"THE FABLES OF AESOP": THE *COLLECTIO AUGUSTANA*

In the *Aesop Romance*, the hero lectures to the young man he had adopted in Babylon on the correct conduct for his dealings with other people in life (chaps. 109–110). The speech, like the other chapters in section 4 of the vita (chaps. 101–123), is adapted from a corresponding passage in the *Ahikar Romance*. In the Greek version, however, one particular 'Aesopic' method of handing out good advice is missing, although it is method which—as we may infer from an Aramaic *Ahikar* papyrus written in the fifth century B.C. (see Oettinger 1992, 13)—the source text employed for roughly a quarter of the speech in question: illustrating a moral precept by way of a fable. Why would the author of the *Aesop Romance* choose to have the λογοποιός keeping his fables to himself here? One plausible explanation could lie in the form of presentation used in the source at this point. The fables in Ahikar's speech are not applied to specific situations, but strung together in series as moral instruction for the recipient, in the way a fable book would present its texts. And within "The Life and Fables of Aesop" this form would have been reserved for the second part.

Can this noticeable omission of Ahikar's catalog-style fables and maxims be taken as one further indication that it was the author of the "biographical" part in "The Life and Fables of Aesop" who first linked the fable book—the one, that is, which survives today in the shape of the *Collectio Augustana*—with the *Vita Aesopi*? Assuming that this was so (and there are good reasons for doing just that) then we may also venture to suggest that the fables in the original version of the *Collectio Augustana* were probably compiled by an author who, like Babrius, was familiar with Mesopotamian fable literature. If true, this would explain one feature which Babrius's fable book and the *Collectio Augustana* have in common, namely, that the texts in the prose collection and the poems in the *Mythiambi* are arranged in alphabetical order. We have already seen that Sumerian collections from the second millennium B.C. were alphabetical (supra, p. 53), and so it seems logical to assume that this structural principle was also applied in the original version of the *Collectio Augustana*. The next step is, then, to consider how the author of the "Fables of Aesop" handled this traditional component.

Clearly it must be taken into account here that a prose fable book is much more likely to have been altered in content and structure by its successive editors and adapters than a verse collection. The *Augustana*-based collections *rec. Ia, II*, and *III*, which were definitely not compiled until late antiquity and Byzantine times, contain fables not included amongst the 231 texts found in the manuscripts of *rec. I*, and this alone means that we cannot regard the structural outlines visible in the extant codices as a faithful representation of the archetype's configuration. Nevertheless, if the book structure of Phaedrus's *Fabulae Aesopiae* is still perceptible in the five abridged *libri* we have in the *Codex Pithoeanus* (see above, pp. 39 ff.), it is possible that, in certain fable sequences at least, the *Collectio Augustana* can offer us some idea of the original layout. We find there, for example, four stag fables in which the theme "dying protagonist bewails its own unhappy end"—this occurs here for the first time in the collection—is treated in skillful variations (*Aes.* 74–77). These texts come across as a 'tetralogy' and leave us with the distinct impression that they were aligned in this way by the collection's original author and not by a much later Byzantine editor. The same is true, for example, of the five Zeus fables (*Aes.* 105–109), which are elegantly linked by a web of thematic, structural, and stylistic allusions.

The significance of these and other interconnected fables has yet to be properly assessed in studies focusing specifically on such groups. What has already been analyzed in depth is the narrative structure of the individual fables in the *Collectio Augustana*. In his invaluable book M. Nøjgaard (1964–1967) proves, as we saw earlier, that the *Collectio Augustana* is not a collection in the true sense of the word, but actually a fable book conceived by its author as a homogeneous unit (1:131 ff.). With Nøjgaard's findings in mind, let us take a look at one example—*Aes.* 116—of the anonymous Greek author's narrative technique:

> Καρκίνος ἀναβὰς ἀπὸ τῆς θαλάσσης ἐπί τινος αἰγιαλοῦ
> μόνος ἐνέμετο. ἀλώπηξ δὲ λιμώττουσα, ὡς ἐθεάσατο
> αὐτόν, ἀποροῦσα τροφῆς, προσδραμοῦσα συνέλαβεν
> αὐτόν. ὁ δὲ μέλλων καταβιβρώσκεσθαι ἔφη 'ἀλλ᾽ ἔγωγε
> δίκαια πέπονθα, ὅτι θαλάσσιος ὢν χερσαῖος ἠβουλήθην
> γενέσθαι.'
> 5   Οὕτω καὶ τῶν ἀνθρώπων οἱ τὰ οἰκεῖα καταλιπόντες
> ἐπιτηδεύματα καὶ τοῖς μηδὲν προσήκουσιν ἐπιχειροῦντες
> εἰκότως δυστυχοῦσιν.

A crab came up out of the sea, intending now to live alone on the shore. Seeing it, a hungry fox ran after it for want of <other> food and seized it. About to be gobbled up it said: "I truly deserve this fate because I, a seadweller, wanted to become a land-dweller."

Thus too those people who give up their normal occupations and undertake things which do not befit them suffer deservedly.

Typical of most fables in the *Augustana* collection is their balanced structure, and the crab's tale is a case in point. Even proportions are achieved within the narrative here by having each of the fable's three sentences stand for one of the three components: exposition, action proper, and a character's closing remark. This kind of tripartite construction is actually found in many ancient fables from the early stages of the genre onward (see above, p. 20), but the *Collectio Augustana* is the only fable book in which the opening, middle, and closing sections of a narrative are so frequently symmetrical. Leaving aside the twelve etiological fables (*Aes.* 3, 39, 103, 105, 106, 108, 109, 117, 163, 166, 171, 185), the nine "vying-match" fables (*Aes.* 12, 14, 20, 46, 70, 130, 213, 223, 229), the two λόγοι that are pseudo-scientific in content (*Aes.* 118, 218), and *Aes.* 71—a rhetorical pièce de résistance—there are among the remaining 207 of the 231 texts found in our manuscripts 136 which are tripartite in structure. In only 25 fables does the narrative comprise more than three stages, and in their outward form most of these are in fact more like short stories (*Aes.* 1, 9, 28, 31, 50, 53, 57, 73, 84, 89, 90, 101, 134, 142, 145, 150, 162, 165, 170, 172, 173, 180, 181, 200, 210). Each of the 46 fables left after this count consists of two parts, and together they form a group that is, in terms of structural balance, remarkably homogeneous (7, 15, 27, 29, 33, 34, 37, 42, 45, 54, 58, 61, 64, 76, 96, 98, 104, 110, 114, 119, 128, 135, 136, 137, 139, 141, 157, 167, 169, 174, 183, 184, 189, 192, 198, 202, 205, 206, 212, 215, 216, 217, 219, 220, 224, 228).

As in the example above, the action in a number of fables is triggered by an animal's hunger or thirst. The author of the *Collectio Augustana* is also especially fond of having a character catch sight of something (cf. line 2 ὡς ἐθεάσατο; elsewhere also θεασάμενος) and thus set the ball rolling. This can occur in any section of the tripartite narrative; if it occurs in the third, then the figure that "catches sight"—usually one who has only just entered the scene—is prompted by this to utter the closing words (cf., e.g., *Aes.* 56). Remarks commenting on or summarizing the incident constitute the narrative's third part in approximately two-thirds of the texts. They most frequently appear in the form of a reproach made by one character to another because of the latter's behavior, relatively often as the lament of figure suffering some misfortune or about to die—we have just seen one such instance above and shall be returning to this form later and occasionally as an answer to a question. At the end of the incident itself the anonymous author sometimes uses the phrase "And thus it came about that . . ." (οὕτω τε συνέβη . . .), for example, in several of the fables with more than three parts.

The narrative is, then, for the most part simple and unvarying, with a tendency toward the formulaic. Was this premeditated? It does seem very likely that the author deliberately kept the style plain in order to give the texts an air of authenticity. Contemporary readers were supposed to feel that the book before them was "the real Aesop," the work of a man who had written down his λόγοι centuries before, in an age when Greek prose had still been in its baby shoes and its diction not yet swollen with the rhetoric they knew from their own day. "Aesop" could well be imagined to have fallen into a certain monotonous routine when setting down the vast number of fables, even if he had always varied these a little in his oral presentations to suit the occasion. Perhaps the author of the *Collectio Augustana* even planned this fable book as a prose contrast to the one by Babrius. If we compare the two, then the *Mythiambi* appears as an assortment of skillfully embellished tales, while the prose fables seem more like the collected works of a 'professional' fabulist—indeed, of the very man who was traditionally regarded as having established the genre's place in Greek literature. The fact that many fables in the *Collectio Augustana* are related to fables found in Babrius permits more than just the assumption that the poet drew on the prose fable book or that the two authors used the same source. It is equally possible that the author of the *Augustana* collection knew the *Mythiambi*.

The contrast between these prose texts and the verse fables of Babrius, who was generally more interested in content than in potential for moralizing, is also significant when it comes to the following question: can the rule which applies throughout the *Collectio Augustana*—that a fable must always end with an *epimythium*—be presumed to have applied in the archetype as well? If it is true that the original fable book was 'sold' to readers as the genuine Aesopic article—the theory supported in this introduction—then the answer must certainly be in the affirmative. An alleged edition of Aesop would have to have stated explicitly for every fable—not just here and there, as in Babrius's book—the *fabula docet* which the genre's 'Homer' had wanted drawn from the tale. Whether the author of the *Collectio Augustana* knew the poems of Babrius or not, the fable book being presented to the public as the work of Greece's first λογοποιός had to offer as many morals as it did fables. Moreover, the wording of the *epimythia* here includes formulaic expressions, and this fits in with our other observations on the outward appearance of the *Augustana* fables. This phrasing was developed from the conventional openings that introduced the moral in earlier texts, and in terms of this tradition there are two types of *epimythium* distinguishable in the *Collectio Augustana*:

1. The *epimythium* introduced with the formula "So we too must now . . ." (ἄταρ οὖν καὶ ἡμᾶς δεῖ . . . : nine times) or "Thus [fare people who] . . ." (οὕτως . . . : eighty-seven times); these are modeled on the way the *fabula docet* is signaled in fables which serve as exempla ("Thus you too . . ."; supra, p. 20).
2. The *epimythium* introduced with the phrase "The fable applies to [such and such a person] . . ." (οὗτος ὁ λόγος ἁρμόττει πρὸς . . . or similar: fifty times), or "This fable shows/teaches . . ." (ὁ λόγος δηλοῖ/διδάσκει . . . : eighty-five times); these are derived from *promythia* found in the fable *repertoria*, which began to appear in Hellenistic times, as documented by *Papyrus Rylands 493* ("[for a certain type of person] the following fable is applicable"; supra, p. 24).

Given that two forms of *epimythium* are used in the *Collectio Augustana*, one might be tempted to consider whether perhaps the author only took his fable material from two specific types of source text. The fables with type one could have been borrowed from authors who inserted fables into their works in order to illustrate a certain point, those with type two from existing *repertoria*. For one thing, however, we have no way of determining the origins of fables with type two *epimythia*, because the one *repertorium* we could draw on for textual comparison—*Papyrus Rylands 493*—only survives in fragments. For another, an author who, as Nøjgaard (1964–1967, 1:131 ff.) demonstrates, puts a distinct personal stamp on borrowed material in terms of narrative technique and auctorial intentions can obviously also be credited with having opened an *epimythium* with a specific type of phrase not because the source text used it, but because it seemed best suited to the type of moral the fable was now meant to convey. And in any case, the wording of the *epimythia* in our manuscripts might well have been altered by the editing copyists of late antiquity or the Byzantine period.

Once again, then, we find ourselves unable to say with any degree of certainty which sources this author might have turned to for his work. We can merely establish that, like the fable books of Phaedrus and Babrius, this Aesopica collection too contains many fables for which it is our only source. The precise number in this case is 102 (see the apparatus in *CFA*), and if we add to these the 14 Augustana fables otherwise found only in the collections of three Byzantine fabulists—Ignatius Diaconus, "Syntipas," and Rhetor Brancatianus (*Aes.* 13, 60, 69, 76, 86, 97, 120, 147, 149, 184, 192, 201, 219, 228)—we come to a total of 116, which represents almost half of the 231 texts in the *Collectio Augustana*. As in Phaedrus and Babrius, those of the exclusively *Augustana* fables that tend in form toward the comic sketch are the ones most likely to have been the author's own creations. This is an interesting observation here—in the very book which probably constituted the second part of "The Life and Fables of Aesop"—because the earthy humor of some of these yarns is reminiscent of the earthy anecdotes told in the Xanthus section of the *Aesop Romance* (chaps. 20–91); *Aes.* 57, 89, 95, and 170 illustrate this similarity well.

Another instance of analogy between the *Collectio Augustana* and the *Aesop Romance* merits our attention at this point. We have already seen in the former the type of fable where the narrative ends with a protagonist lamenting his or her unhappy lot. The text quoted above (*Aes.* 116) represents, together with 8 other fables, one of two variants in this kind: about to die a violent death, the lamenting character acknowledges that it deserves no better (using the formulaic phrase δίκαια πάσχω or similar; cf. *Aes.* 77, 120, 148, 176, 181, 187, 203, 209). In the other variant, of which there are 10 examples, the doomed figure merely calls out "unhappy me!" (ἄθλιος ἔγωγε or similar; cf. *Aes.* 25, 74, 75, 76, 80, 86, 115, 128, 131, 147). Phaedrus and Babrius also know this type of fable (cf. for instance Phaedr. 1.12 and Babr. 43 with *Aes.* 74), but the author of the *Collectio Augustana* uses it considerably more often, and 13 of 19 such texts (we could also include *Aes.* 139 and 144 here, which are both without extant parallel versions) are only found in this fable book.

Now, to return to our analogy, just as in almost all of these 19 *Augustana* fables the narrative can be divided into the three parts—exposition, action proper, and final lament—in the *Aesop Romance* too three stages can be distinguished—we noted these earlier—and the sequence there is similar to the arrangement in the fables just considered. In chapters 1–19 Aesop is endowed by the Muses with the gift of λογοποιία, in 20–123 he uses this to his own advantage and detriment, and in 124–141 his abuse of the gift leads to his death. Having begun—before his (literal) fall—to suspect that nothing will save him, he twice makes remarks which are at least faintly reminiscent of the words uttered by doomed characters in Augustana fables. Shortly after his arrest Aesop cries out: "How shall I, a mortal, manage to escape what is in store for me now?" (chap. 128.11: νῦν ἐγὼ θνητὸς ὤν πῶς δυνήσομαι τὸ μέλλον ἐκφυγεῖν;). And to a friend—one who only turns up now, near the end of the novel, and who can therefore be compared to the fable characters whom Nøjgaard terms *le survenant* ("the newcomer")—Aesop says: "Any sense I had left I lost when I set out for Delphi" (chap. 131.16–17: ἀπώλεσα . . . καὶ ὃν πρῶτον εἶχον νοῦν εἰς Δελφοὺς εἰσελθών). The crab in *Aes.* 116 reproaches itself in strikingly similar fashion for having wanted to give up its natural habitat.

Here we have, then, two 'tragic' narratives, and each is unfolded in three stages. The one is told within the space of a short fable. The other is spread over the course of a fictional vita devoted to the most famous of all fabulists, a man whose unnatural death was mentioned as early as the fifth century B.C. (*Test.* 20 Perry), but whose 'biography' as we know it—the *Vita Aesopi,* or *Aesop Romance,* that is—was not written until the second/third century A.D. Dare we infer again that the author of this novel also wrote the fable book that now survives in the form of the *Collectio Augustana*? Even if thorough investigation of the whole question should reveal that the two books must have been created by two different authors, one result of this discussion will still stand: a three-stage unfolding of events is characteristic of both narrators. When compared with the Aesopica in the *Augustana* collection, where the final lament of each hapless character is preceded by an exposition and the action proper, the triptych presented in the *Aesop Romance*—chapters 1–19, 20–123, and 124–142—reads like a fable spun out to the length of an ancient novel.

The vita and the fable book have one further feature in common, this being that both devote considerable space to a goal otherwise most frequently pursued in satirical literature: the exposure of discrepancies between appearance and reality. We have already noted the importance of this theme within the *Aesop Romance* (see above, pp. 83–84), and in the *Collectio Augustana* its underlying presence can also be felt in many of the fables. Moreover, it is handled here, as indicated earlier (supra, p. 27), with a degree of sarcasm that calls Lucian to mind. Just as those of the satirist's characters who give themselves over to some delusion, or who delude others, are brought down to earth with a bump or mercilessly unmasked, so too the *Augustana* characters who have fallen victim to some illusion, or who lie and cheat, have to face the harsh realities of life. An example of this is found in *Aes.* 121:

Κιθαρῳδὸς ἀφυὴς ἐν κεκονιαμένῳ οἴκῳ συνεχῶς ᾄδων, ἀντηχούσης αὐτῷ τῆς φωνῆς, ᾠήθη ἑαυτὸν εὔφωνον εἶναι σφόδρα. καὶ δὴ ἐπαρθεὶς ἐπὶ τούτῳ ἔγνω δεῖν καὶ εἰς θέατρον εἰσελθεῖν. ἀφικόμενος δὲ ἐπὶ σκηνὴν καὶ πάνυ κακῶς ᾄδων λίθοις βαλλόμενος ἐξηλάθη.

5 Οὕτω καὶ τῶν ῥητόρων ἔνιοι ἐν σχολαῖς εἶναί τινες δοκοῦντες, ὅταν ἐπὶ τὰς πολιτείας ἀφίκωνται, οὐδενὸς ἄξιοι εὑρίσκονται.

An untalented singer sang all the time in a whitewashed room, and because his voice resounded there sonorously, he believed that he had a marvelous singing voice. And since he was now extremely proud of this, he decided that he should perform in the theater too. But when he stood up on the stage and sang dreadfully, he had stones thrown at him and was chased away.

So too some rhetors who enjoy a certain reputation in schools are found to be incompetent when they enter politics.

The frequency with which appearances are contrasted with the realities of life in both the *Aesop Romance* and the *Collectio Augustana* obviously cannot be used as an argument in favor of attributing both books to the same author—destroying illusions is, after all, for a great many ancient writers a fundamental objective. The time has therefore come to end our comparison of the themes shared by both works, indeed to end our musings on "The Life and Fables of Aesop." Faced with the harsh realities of manuscript traditions, we may just allow ourselves a final, brief lament: what a great pity it is that this book has not survived in its original form!

* * *

While no surveys of work on Greek (prose) fable collections have ever been compiled, there is now one comprehensive bibliography of literature on the *Aesop Romance:* Beschorner and Holzberg (1992); studies from the 1990s are discussed in Holzberg (1999). The text of *Vita G* is edited by Perry (1952), Papathomopoulos (1991 [2d ed., quoted here in this introduction] but cf. the reviews by Haslam 1992 and van Dijk 1994b), and Ferrari (1997). Translations of this version (supplemented with textual material from *Vita W*) can be found in Daly (1961a; reprint: Hansen 1998, 106–162), Poethke (1974), Ferrari (1997), and Wills (1997, 181–215). *Vita W* is edited by Westermann (1845), Perry (1952), and Papathomopoulos (1999a; cf. also his edition of five early Greek translations of the *Aesop Romance* [1999b]). *Vita Pl* is included in Eberhard (1872), and papyrus texts from the novel appear in Zeitz (1935), Perry (1936), and Haslam (1980–1986). Indispensable for work on the very poorly transmitted text of *Vita G* are the index (for Perry 1952) by Dimitriadou-Toufexi (1981), the summary of all previous textual criticism by Papathomopoulos (1989), the articles by Ferrari (1995a and b), the analyses of the novel's language by Birch (1955) and Hostetter (1955), and the studies on its textual history by Marc (1910), Perry (1933, 1936, 1952, 1–32, and 1966), and Hower (1936). General (albeit mostly source-oriented) studies are Zeitz (1936), Hausrath (1940, 114–140), La Penna (1962), Holbek (1977), Adrados (1979, 1979–1987, 1:661–697, and 1999a, 647–685), Jedrkiewicz (1989, 39–215), Giannattasio Andria (1995), and Hägg (1997). In those studies devoted to a reading of the fables as a whole—Patterson (1991, 13–43), Holzberg (1993 and 1996), Luzzatto (1996b), Ferrari (1997, 5–55), Ludwig (1997), and Pervo (1998)—the focus is on the extant texts. Useful reading on the question of sources includes Wiechers (1961), Winkler (1985, 276–291), and Luzzatto (1988); the following is also valuable on the relationship between the *Aesop* and *Ahikar* romances: Meyer (1912), Conybeare, Harris, and Lewis (1913), Hausrath (1918), Degen (1977), Lindenberger (1985), Gómez (1990), Wilsdorf (1991), Oettinger (1992), Kussl (1992), Luzzatto (1992 and 1994), Fales (1993), and Marinčič (1995). Various aspects of the novel's literary and philosophical contexts are discussed by Jedrkiewicz (1990–1992, 1994a and b, 1997), Brodersen (1992), Merkle (1992), Mignogna (1992), Schauer and Merkle (1992), and Papademetriou (1997, 13–42). The thoughts on the narrative structure found in Holzberg (1992b; cf. van Dijk 1994a) and summarized in this introduction are partly modified, partly corrected by van Dijk (1995b), Merkle (1996), and Shiner (1998). The first steps toward a sociohistorical interpretation are undertaken by Hopkins (1993), Hägg (1997), and Ragone (1997); allusions to contemporary cults (Dionysus, Isis) are traced by von Möllendorf (1994) and Dillery (1999), while Wills (1997, 23 ff.), Pervo (1998, 97 ff.), Shiner (1998), and Pesce and Destro (1999) draw parallels to the Gospels in terms of form and intellectual background. On the book's lively *Nachleben* see Patterson (1991), Beschorner (1992), Hilpert (1992), Holzberg (1993), Pillolla (1994), Ludwig (1997), and Papademetriou (1997).

The various editions of the *Collectio Augustana,* and the collections based on this, are introduced above, pp. 5–6, together with details of existing translations, so that here we need only mention the relevant index by Garcia and Lopez (1991). Literature on these collections is devoted almost exclusively to their textual history and usually includes attempts to date the texts and to analyze their language and style: see Hausrath (1894 and 1901)—Hausrath remained convinced that the fables in the *Collectio Augustana* resulted mostly from the exercises students of rhetoric were set in imperial times—Marc (1910), Perry (1936 and 1952, 295–311), and Adrados (1948, 1952, 1969–1970, 1979–1987, 1984, 1992, and 2000). Adrados dates the *Collectio Augustana* to the fourth/fifth century A.D. and tries to trace it back, via a "Prae-Augustana" (ca. A.D. 100) and an "ur-Augustana" (second century B.C.), to a collection of fables written in iambic trimeters. The arguments, however, are as unconvincing as those of Luzzatto (1983), who dates the *Collectio Augustana* to the tenth century A.D.: she contends—unmistakably influenced by the very theories she rejects, that is, those of Adrados—that the fables represent the remains of "political" Byzantine poetry. An actual interpretation of the fables themselves is offered at some length by Nøjgaard (1964–1967, 1:131–419); compare also his discussion of their literary-historical context (480 ff.), a section of the book which proved to be very valuable during the preparation of this chapter.

The ethical message of the *Augustana Collection* is discussed by Zafiropoulos (2001).

* * *

■ *Aesopus Latinus*

Not only Greek-speaking readers were given the opportunity, at some point under the empire, to become acquainted with the "real" Aesop; Latin audiences were also offered the 'genuine article' in the form of the *Aesopus Latinus.* Writing probably in the fourth century, its anonymous author prefaced the fables with a fictitious letter of dedication (p. 4–6 Th.) from "Aesop" to a certain Rufus (Xanthus, the fabulist's master in the vita?); readers were thus invited to believe that these really were the tales invented by the genre's founder. And, just in case this was not proof enough of the collection's authenticity, two of the four *recensiones* in which the *Aesopus Latinus* has come down to us produce another letter by way of corroboration. Placed before the dedicatory epistle, it purports to be from one Romulus to his son Tiberinus (p. 2–3 Th.), and its supposed writer claims to have translated the fables into Latin from the Greek of Aesop. Both letters are quite obviously literary forgeries, each pieced none too skillfully together from Phaedrus. Snatches of his wording were borrowed from the prologues and epilogues in the *Fabulae Aesopiae*, and some were used twice, so that the two letters—both devoted principally to the usefulness of the fables for the addressee—echo each other at times. And the first fable following these epistles, "The Cockerel and the Pearl," is a prose adaptation of Phaedrus 3.2.

At this point, if not before, the reader begins to suspect that the *Aesopus Latinus* is in fact a prose version of Phaedrus, and what then follows seems to bear out this impression. In the *recensio Gallicana* (one of the two manuscript traditions with "Romulus's" prefatory letter; the other, the *recensio vetus,* differs only in that it has no parallel versions to Phaedrus 2.18, 4.15, 17, and 19 [= 48, 89, 91, 93 Th.])—forty-seven of its eighty-one fables soon reveal themselves as adaptations of forty-seven Phaedrian fables found in the *Codex Pithoeanus* and the *Appendix Perottina.* A further eight prove, when compared with the corresponding texts in the collection which we know from the eleventh-century copy made by Ademar of Chabannes (supra, p. 4), to be Phaedrian in origin as well. The *Ademar Codex* contains—in addition to twenty-nine fables which belong to a third *recensio* of the *Aesopus Latinus,* and eight of unknown origin—thirty fables that are the result of a more or less mechanical 'prosification' of thirty poems by Phaedrus. Eight of these were based on textual versions which were also used by the author of the *Aesopus Latinus* for eight fables (cf. nos. 4, 15, 22, 51, 53, 54, 63, 92 Th.). This cannot actually be proved conclusively, because the eight source texts in question, together with those of three other fables (41, 82, 84 Th.), no longer exist. However, it is a reasonable assumption, given the close resemblance between these eleven prose adaptations and the nineteen for which we do have the Phaedrus's versions.

So far, then, we have fifty-five fables in the *recensio Gallicana* of "Romulus" which we can confidently trace back to Phaedrus. Identification of the sources for the remaining twenty-six, by contrast, is not always clear-cut. Nevertheless, one observation does allow us to form a certain picture of this 'Romulan' collection's genesis. The last of its four books begins with five fables which are definitely of Phaedrian origin (= 71–75 Th.), but there follow three which we only know from "Romulus" and which were very probably not based on Phaedrian texts (= 76–78 Th.); then come two fables which, in spite of their thematic similarity to two of the *Fabulae Aesopiae,* bear absolutely no resemblance to those versions (= 79 and 83 Th.), and seven fables (= 85–91 Th.) which correspond almost word for word to seven fables in Ps.-Dositheus's bilingual schoolbook (supra, pp. 30–31); only at the end of book 4 do we find another three texts that can probably all be classified as adaptations of Phaedrian fables (= 92, 94, and 95 Th.), with one more from Ps.-Dositheus inserted between them (= 93 Th.). So, thirteen fables in book 4 of "Romulus's" *Aesopus Latinus* are without question, or in all likelihood, not Phaedrian in origin. In the other thirteen of the twenty-six yet to be 'placed'— one of these is in book 4 (= 94 Th., just mentioned), the rest are scattered over books 1–3 (= 21, 23, 24, 35, 36, 39, 52, 55, 56, 64, 66, and 70 Th.)—there are clear indications that their prose is a 'translation' of Phaedrian verse. Summing up, we can say that the *Aesopus Latinus* which "Romulus" claims to be the result of his translating is not a straightforward prose version of Phaedrus;

the first sixty-five of its fables were created by adapting Phaedri-ana, and to these was added a block which comprised new versions of fables taken from various authors (in three cases again from Phaedrus). Or, in other words, sixty-eight of the eighty-one fables in the *recensio Gallicana* would appear to be adaptations of Phaedrian fables.

Turning to the fourth *recensio* within the *Aesopus Latinus* tradition, we find evidence which suggests that the fable book existed before "Romulus's" compilation in a version which consisted of fables based exclusively on poems from Phaedrus, and that this earlier collection was probably the archetype for all versions of the book. The fourth *recensio,* which survives in a tenth-century codex from Wissembourg, Alsace (*Gud. lat. 148* in Wolfenbüttel), differs in four important aspects from "Romulus's" version.

1. It opens with only one letter of dedication, "Aesop's"; this is divided into two and frames the fables; the second portion of the epistle includes as insertion the prose adaptation of "The Cockerel and the Pearl" (Phaedrus 3.2), which opens "Romulus's" fable book.
2. As in Phaedrus, the fables here are divided into five *libri,* and the first text in the first *liber* is, again as in the poet's work, "The Wolf and the Lamb."
3. The *recensio* contains in all fifty-eight fables; two of these, which also appear in "Romulus's" *recensio vetus,* are not prose adaptations of Phaedriana but merely 'prosifications,' like thirty of the texts in the *Ademar Codex;* they therefore cannot be counted as *Aesopus Latinus* fables. In all, thirty-nine of the texts are proven adaptations from Phaedrus, and the remaining seventeen—like the corresponding fables in "Romulus"—are almost certainly based on poems in the *Fabulae Aesopiae.*
4. The texts here are very similar to their counterparts in "Romulus," but, in cases where we still have Phaedrus's poems, comparison reveals numerous passages where the original text is rendered more faithfully in the *Wissembourg Codex* than in the two "Romulus" *recensiones.*

These findings combine to form the following picture of the fable book's textual history. The original work consisted of five *libri* and was prefaced only with "Aesop's" letter. It was probably written around A.D. 350; Thiele (1910) considers this the earliest possible date for linguistic reasons, and it would seem acceptable because it allows a suitable gap between this version and the one by "Romulus," whose *terminus ante quem* is generally believed to have been the year 500 (cf. above, p. 64, on Ausonius's possibly relevant note). The ur-"Aesopus" was nothing more than a prose Phaedrus, the author of which selected only fables which seemed particularly 'Aesopic' in content, that is, fables in which at least one animal played a part (one exception is in the *Wissembourg Codex*: 4.1 = 60 Th., from Phaedrus, *Appendix Perottina* 29). An anonymous author rewrote the fable book, supplementing it with tales adapted from other sources, and decided, in addition, to create the fiction that this work was offering the legendary fables of Aesop in the Latin translation once produced by a famous Roman. After all, which eminent Romulus with a son called Tiberinus could the anonymous of late antiquity have meant? Surely only Rome's founding father! If this is so, then our unknown author was trying to authenticate a literary work with credentials which reached even further back into the imperial past than those presented by "Dictys" and "Dares," for the reliability of whose Trojan War accounts the names Nero in the one case, and in the other Sallust and Nepos stand as guarantee.

Anyone attempting to interpret the fables in the *Aesopus Latinus* faces at the outset two major stumbling blocks. First, as research stands today—the focus has always been primarily on reconstructions of lost Phaedriana—we cannot say for certain which of the fables passed down in the book's four *recensiones* stood in the original version. The manuscript traditions for "Romulus" offer (in the one) twelve and (in the other) eleven Phaedrus-based fables which are missing in the *Wissembourg Codex,* and there are two possible explanations for this. Either the version in this codex only represents an epitome of the original, or "Romulus" added the twelve adaptations from Phaedrus to the ur-"Aesopus" along with the texts adapted from other authors. Precisely which fables the original did contain is a problem closely connected with the question of book structure. The order in which the five *libri* of the *Wissembourg Codex* arranges its fables differs from the order in the four *libri* of "Romulus," and yet certain principles are perceptible in both lineups, even just on first reading. The beginning of the first book in each provides a good example of this. In the *Wissembourg Codex* the fables 1–4 (= 3, 5, 4, 35 Th.) clearly stand as two pairs— one is reminded here of M. J. Luzzatto's observations on Avianus (1984; supra, p. 65); in "Romulus" the first and 'programmatic' fable (= 1 Th.) is followed by four (2–5 = 3–6 Th.) which are alternately linked in theme (*abab*, schematically speaking). But which *recensio* has retained, here and for the rest of the fables, the original book structure?

The other major difficulty confronting us lies in the different wording found in the various manuscript versions of the same fables, and also in the extremely poor quality of some of the codices. The *Wissembourg Codex* in particular presents insurmountable obstacles, numerous passages having apparently been mangled beyond intelligibility by a copyist of somewhat indifferent language skills. We find there, as G. Thiele puts it (1910), "a Latin in the grip of total decomposition" (clvii); moreover, although this very *recensio* is especially important for a reconstruction of the original fable book, it is still not available in the form of a satisfactory historical-critical edition, as Thiele neglected to note in his apparatus the variant readings added by a correcting hand ("W²"). So, if we are wondering what intentions the author of the *Aesopus Latinus* may have had, and decide, in the hope of establishing significant deviations, to compare fables there with their source versions, which text should we use? It is very doubtful whether there is any chance of determining which *recensio* is most closely akin to the original. Perhaps one day a textual critic will tackle the problem with his wishful-thinking cap in the closet. Until that happens, all that we can do, if we still want to take a step—tentative as it may be—toward interpreting the *Aesopus Latinus,* is the following: to examine those fables that are included in at least three *recensiones* and that have essentially the same content in each, in order to establish whether and how they deviate from the source texts.

Having said that, we shall now be looking at one such fable— and subsequently reviewing the conclusions so far permissible from this kind of analysis—but of necessity without considering all available *recensiones* of the text: we simply do not have the room. The fable in question—"The Crow and the Fox" (19 Th.), of which we have already seen Phaedrus's version (supra, pp. 42 ff.)— is only quoted here in a form based on manuscripts from the *recensio Gallicana;* for the rest readers are referred to Thiele's synoptical edition (1910).

> *Qui se laudari gaudent verbis subdolis, decepti paeni-*
> *tent. de quibus similis est fabula.*
> *Cum de fenestra corvus caseum raperet, alta consedit in*
> *arbore. vulpis ut hunc vidit, e contra sic ait corvo: 'O*
> 5   *corve, quis similis tibi? et pennarum tuarum quam mag-*
> *nus est nitor! qualis decor tuus est! et si vocem habuisses*
> *claram, nulla tibi prior avis fuisset.' at ille dum vult*
> *placere vulpi et vocem suam ostendere, validius sursum*
> *clamavit et ore patefacto oblitus caseum deiecit. quem*
> *celeriter vulpis dolosa avidis rapuit dentibus. tunc corvus*
> *ingemuit et stupore deceptum se paenituit. sed post*
> *irreparabile damnum quid iuvat paenitere?*

People who are pleased when praised in words full of guile regret this when they have been deceived. For such persons this fable is appropriate.

After a crow had stolen cheese from a window-sill, he perched upon a high tree. When a fox saw him, he spoke thus to the crow: "O crow, who can compare to you? How great is the gloss of your feather! What beauty is yours! And if you had a clear voice, no bird would come before you!" Now the other, being anxious to please the fox and demonstrate his voice, called out rather loudly on high and, forgetting the cheese, dropped it as he opened his beak. This the crafty fox swiftly seized upon with his greedy fangs. Then the crow sighed and regretted having allowed himself in his foolishness to be cheated. But what good is regret after irreversible damage?

In its language this fable is similar to most of the other Phaedriana adaptations we find in the *Aesopus Latinus.* The poet's diction is partly adopted without change and partly blended with the Latin of late antiquity; very occasionally a longer phrase is replaced with an expression completely foreign to the original in style. On the one hand, characteristic elements of Vulgar Latin grammar pervade Phaedrus's *sermo urbanus*—here for example the pluperfect subjunctive in a conditional clause where one would expect the imperfect subjunctive (line 6); on the other, Phaedrus's style is almost entirely stripped of its comical effect, which, as we saw above, is at times achieved by the use of epic phraseology—*ingemuit corvi deceptus stupor,* for instance, is turned into the comparatively trivial sounding *corvus ingemuit et stupore deceptum se paenituit.* Nevertheless, this cross between Phaedrus's iambic poetry and simple narrative prose produced something which, with its curious discordance, is not entirely void of charm.

The *fabula docet* in our example is conveyed in a form that is not particularly typical of the whole *Aesopus Latinus.* Here we have a *promythium,* but, instead of an *epimythium,* we are given merely a closing auctorial remark phrased as the narrator's rhetorical question. The majority of fables in the *Aesopus Latinus* have both a *promythium* and an *epimythium* (cf. the chapter "The Morals" in Thiele 1910, lxxii ff.). In many cases where the *promythium* in the Phaedrian source had derived a general moral truth from the story, this is retained without much alteration, and the corresponding *epimythium* then comprises a maxim which alludes specifically to the incident narrated; for instance, in "The Frog and the Bull" (= 50 Th.), which the author—like Phaedrus—uses to advise against *imitatio* of *potentes* (Phaedr. 1.24.1 ~ *recensio Gallicana* [here] lines 1–3), the closing words are "Don't you puff yourself up in case you burst" (*noli te inflare, ne crepes*).

The *Aesopus Latinus* version of "The Crow and the Fox" supplements the original text slightly at two points. The fox's speech is a little more verbose here than in Phaedrus, and when the crow opens its beak to sing and drops the cheese, the prose author tries to explain its involuntary moves more precisely—in slow motion, as it were. These two forms of amplification are characteristic of the anonymous fabulist's work. An unmistakable desire to display familiarity with the *ars rhetorica* has resulted in the occasional embellishment or even alteration of direct speech. Thus the four verses of friendly advice offered by a faithful dog to a thief in Phaedrus 1.23 have become more of a sermon in the *Aesopus Latinus* (29, §2–8 Th.). And, as Phaedrus often expected readers to use their imagination for additional detail, the author of the *Aesopus Latinus* frequently feels the need to fill in the 'gaps'; a good example here is his adaptation of "Town Mouse and Country Mouse," as compared to the prose rendering of

Phaedrus's lost poem in the *Ademar Codex* (= 15 Th.).

At times, the original sequence of events presented in the fables has been changed so much in the narrative sections of *Aesopus Latinus* texts that they virtually constitute new fables (13, 28, 31 Th.; cf. also 10, 44, 59, 68 Th.). This observation prompted Thiele (1910) to advance a theory regarding the genesis of the "Romulus" collection, a theory which shows his thinking to be deeply rooted in nineteenth-century source fixations. The fables which deviate in content from their Phaedrian originals, together with the texts in the fourth book which can neither have been taken from Ps.-Dositheus, nor have been created as adaptations of Phaedriana (see above, pp. 96–97), came—argued Thiele— from a lost "Aesopus Latinus." This he dated back to the second century A.D. and identified as the translation of a now similarly lost collection of Greek Aesopica. Not only did he believe his reconstructed "Aesopus Latinus" to have been the source for non-Phaedrian fables and for those which deviate considerably in content from their corresponding Phaedrian versions, but he also thought that *Aesopus Latinus* texts which contain just slightly more detail than their Phaedrian counterparts must be the results of "contamination," that is, of combining in each case a poem by Phaedrus with a text from the Thielean "Aesopus Latinus."

It is always perplexing to see how profoundly influenced earlier generations of classics scholars were by Romantic and historicist thought, which determined their notions of Latin literary production and blinded them to what now seems obvious and plausible. In studies on the fourth-century *Aesopus Latinus*—like those on a great many works of Roman literature—one possibility was never even considered, although it is an explanation which, when a literary adaptation displays notable deviations from its source, really ought to be the first that comes to mind. To be specific: could such divergence not be the result of changes which the adapting author *wanted* to make, and should we not, therefore, first establish whether the differences can perhaps be explained as part of this same author's conception of the work? If we read the *Aesopus Latinus* fables—both those in "Romulus" and those in the *Wissembourg Codex*—in one sitting and with an open mind, then it becomes clear, even prior to any analytic evaluation of our observations, that the author of this fable book adapted the poems from Phaedrus strictly according to certain criteria.

Sad to say, no one has yet published a study in which these criteria are set forth on the basis of careful textual collation, and this introductory chapter is obviously not going to be able to remedy the situation. Interested students must content themselves for the moment with the one attempt made so far to shed some objective light on the intentions of this fable book's author: two short sections in K. Grubmüller's book on medieval German fables (1977, 62–64, 184–186). Fortunately for us, Grubmüller deviates briefly from his normal field of study—German literature—in order to compare the *Aesopus Latinus* versions of "The Wolf and the Lamb" and "The Lion's Share" (3 and 8 Th.) with their counterparts in Phaedrus (1.1 and 5); he demonstrates that Phaedrus's severe condemnation of coercion and arbitrary wielding of power is considerably diluted in the prose texts. This is a tendency displayed in other *Aesopus Latinus* fables too (cf. esp. 5, 11, 17, 20, 27, 28 Th.). Inevitably, however, attempts to establish the significance of this, that is, in terms of possible intentions underlying the original "Aesopus Latinus," are in many cases hampered by obstacles which lie in the nature of the textual tradition. Comparing, by way of example, the *promythia* in Phaedrus 2.6 and *Aesopus Latinus* 17 Th., we find in the former version (v. 1–3):

> *Contra potentes nemo est munitus satis;*
> *Si vero accessit consiliator maleficus,*
> *Vis et nequitia quicquid oppugnant, ruit.*

No one is sufficiently fortified against the powerful; but if an evildoing adviser joins with such, whatever is besieged by force and rascality combined is sure to fall.

In "Romulus" the social criticism voiced in these lines is substantially modified; the text there says: *qui tutus et munitus est, a malo consiliatore subverti potest* (*recensio Gallicana:* "He who is protected and secure can be brought down by a bad adviser"). In the *Wissembourg Codex,* by contrast, we read: *Contra potentem nemo tutus [quam] si accedet consiliator malus* ("Against someone with power no one is safe if an evil adviser enters the scene"). So, what did the original text have to say here?

To return to the very first sentence in this introduction, the land of the ancient fable lies in ruins. We have picked our way through it now and done our best not only to start clearing the debris, but also to signpost new paths for the future. The task remains, however, colossal.

* * *

Work on the *Aesopus Latinus* has so far only been recorded in connection with discussions of Phaedrus studies (see above, pp. 50 ff.). The relevant texts are edited in Hervieux (1893–1894) and Thiele (1910), and, more specifically, the *Ademar Codex* fables in Thiele (1905) and Bertini (1975). On textual history and text-source relationships, see Zander (1897), Thiele (1905 and 1910), Getzlaff (1907), Zander (1921), Hausrath (1938, 1482–1486), Nøjgaard (1964–1967, 2:404–431), Adrados (1979–1987, 2:473–509, 1999a, 515–558, and 1999b, 9 [this last on a papyrus paraphrase of Phaedrus 1.4]), Gatti (1979), Boldrini (1990a–c and 1991a and b), and Henderson (1999, 321–329), whose theories for a reconstruction of the *Aesopus Latinus* differ from those presented in the above chapter here. A useful survey of all questions raised by this text is offered by Grubmüller (1977, 61–67); Huber (1990, 83–91) interprets fable 59 Th.

REFERENCES

For further literature on texts discussed here, see Carnes 1985 and Beschorner 1997.

Adrados, F. R. 1948. *Estudios sobre el léxico de las fábulas Esópicas: En torno a los problemas de la koiné litteraria.* Salamanca: Consejo Superior de Investigaciones Cientificas.

———. 1952. "El Papiro Rylands 493 y la tradición fabulística antigua." *Emérita* 20:337–388.

———. 1953. Review of Perry 1952. *Gnomon* 25:323–328.

———. 1957. Review of Hausrath 1940–1956. *Gnomon* 29:431–437.

———. 1964. "El tema del águila, de la épica acadia a Esquilo." *Emérita* 32:267–282.

———. 1965. "El tema del léon en el Agamemnón de Esquilo (717–749)." *Emérita* 33:1–5.

———. 1965–1970. Review of Nøjgaard 1964–1967. *Gnomon* 37:540–544; 42:43–49.

———. 1969–1970. "La tradición fabulística griega y sus modelos métricos." *Emérita* 37:235–315; 38:1–52.

———. 1979. "The 'Life of Aesop' and the Origins of Novel in Antiquity." *Quaderni Urbinati di Cultura Classica* 30, n.s., 1:93–112.

———. 1979–1987. *Historia de la fábula greco-latina.* Vol. 1, *Introducción y de los origines a la edad helenística.* Vol. 2, *La fábula en epoca imperial romana y medieval.* Vol. 3, *Inventario y documentación de la fábula greco-latina.* Madrid: Editorial de la Universidad Complutense. [Cf. review by Nøjgaard (1986).]

———. 1984. "Les collections de fables à l'époque hellénistique et romaine." In *La fable: Huit exposés sui vis de discussions,* edited by F. R. Adrados and O. Reverdin, 137–195. Entretiens sur l'Antiquité Classique, no. 30. Geneva: Fondation Hardt.

———. 1992. "La fecha de la Augustana y la tradición fabulística antigua y bizantina." *Prometheus* 18:139–149.

———. 1994. "La fábula en Horacio y su poesía." *Myrtia* 9:131–151.

———. 1999a. *History of the Graeco-Roman Fable.* Vol. 1, *Introduction and From the Origins to the Hellenistic Age.* Translated by L. A. Ray. Mnemosyne, Supplement 201, no. 1. Leiden, Boston, and Cologne: Brill.

———. 1999b. "Nuevos testimonios papiráceos de fábulas esópicas." *Emérita* 67:1–11.

———. 2000. *History of the Graeco-Roman Fable.* Vol. 2, *The Fable during the Roman Empire and in the Middle Ages.* Translated by L. A. Ray. Mnemosyne, Supplement 201, no. 2. Leiden, Boston, and Cologne: Brill.

Adrados, F. R., and O. Reverdin, eds. 1984. *La fable: Huit exposés suivis de discussions.* Entretiens sur l'Antiquité Classique, no. 30. Geneva: Fondation Hardt.

Bajoni, M. G. 1997. "Un esempio di autoapologia in Phaedrus, III, 1?" *Antiquité Classique* 66:289–291.

———. 1999. "Il tempo dello schiavo: alcune osservazioni a Phaedr. 5.8." *Philologus* 143:247–258.

Barabino, G. 1981. "Osservazioni sul senario giambico di Fedro." In δέσμος κοινωνίας: *Scritti di Filologia e Filosofia,* edited by G. Fabiano and E. Salvaneschi, 89–122. Genoa: Melangolo.

Bellonzi, F. 1973. "Fedro e i diritti della fantasia." *Studi Romani* 21:61–63.

Bernardi Perini, G. 1992. "'Cui reddidi iampridem quicquid debui': Il debito di Fedro con Esopo secondo Fedro." In *La storia, la lettera e l'arte a Roma da Tiberio a Domiziano. Atti del Convegno (Mantova, Teatro Accademico 4–5–6–7 ottobre 1990),* 43–59. Mantua: Publi-Paolini.

Bertini, F. 1975. *Il monaco Ademaro e la sua raccolta di favole fedriane.* Genoa: Tilgher.

———. 1981. "Fortuna medievale ed umanistica della favola dell' asino e del cinghiale (Phaedr. I 29)." In *Letterature comparate. Problemi e metodo. Studi in onore di E. Paratore,* 1063–1073. Bologna: Patron.

Beschorner, A. 1992. "Zu Arnolt Bronnens 'Aisopos.'" In *Der Äsop-Roman: Motivgeschichte und Erzählstruktur,* edited by N. Holzberg, 155–161. Classica Monacensia, no. 6. Tübingen: Gunter Narr Verlag.

———. 1997. "Bibliographie." In *Fabeln der Antike: Griechisch-Lateinisch-Deutsch,* edited by H. C. Schnur, 344–362. Düsseldorf and Zurich: Artemis.

Beschorner, A., and N. Holzberg. 1992. "A Bibliography of the Aesop Romance." In *Der Äsop-Roman: Motivgeschichte und Erzählstruktur,* edited by N. Holzberg, 165–187. Classica Monacensia, no. 6. Tübingen: Gunter Narr Verlag.

Bieber, D. 1906. "Studien zur Geschichte der Fabel in den ersten Jahrhunderten der Kaiserzeit." Diss., Munich.

Birch, C. M. 1955. *Traditions of the Life of Aesop.* Ph.D. diss., Washington University, St. Louis.

Bloomer, W. M. 1997. *Latinity and Literary Society at Rome.* Philadelphia: University of Pennsylvania Press. [Esp. 73–109: "The Rhetoric of Freedmen: The Fables of Phaedrus."]

Boldrini, S. 1988. *Fedro e Perotti: Ricerche di storia della tradizione.* Pubblicazioni dell' Università di Urbino. Scienze umane, Serie di linguistica letteratura arte, no. 11. Urbino: Università degli Studi di Urbino.

———. 1990a. "Il codice fedriano modello di Ademaro." In *Memores tui: Studi di letteratura classica ed umanistica in onore di M. Vitaletti,* edited by S. Prete, 11–19. Sassoferrato: Sassoferrato Istituto Internazionale Studi Piceni.

———. 1990b. *Note sulla tradizione manoscritta di Fedro (i tre codici di età carolingia).* Bollettino dei classici, Supplement 9. Rome: Accademia Nazionale dei Lincei.

———. 1990c. "Una testimonianza delle 'favole nuove' di Fedro prima di Perotti: Gualtiero Anglico XLVIII." *Res Publica Litterarum* 13:19–26.

———. 1991a. "Fedro in Ademaro." *Maia* 43:47–49.

———. 1991b. "Il prologo dell'Epitome e la versificazione 'giambica' di Niccolò Perotti." *Res Publica Litterarum* 14:9–18.

Bowra, C. M. 1940. "The Fox and the Hedgehog." *The Classical Quarterly* 34:26–29.

Brodersen, K. 1992. "Rache für Äsop: Zum Umgang mit Geschichte außerhalb der Historiographie." In *Der Äsop-Roman: Motivgeschichte und Erzählstruktur,* edited by N. Holzberg, 97–109. Classica Monacensia, no. 6. Tübingen: Gunter Narr Verlag.

Burkert, W. 1984. *Die orientalisierende Epoche in der griechischen Religion und Literatur.* Sitzungsberichte der Heidelberger Akademie der Wissenschaften, Philosophisch-Historische Klasse, no. 1. Heidelberg: Winter.

Cameron, A. 1967. "Macrobius, Avienus, and Avianus." *The Classical Quarterly,* n.s., 17:385–399.

Carnes, P. 1985. *Fable Scholarship: An Annotated Bibliography.* New York and London: Garland Publishing.

Cascajero, J. 1991. "Lucha de clases e ideología: introducción al estudio de la fábula esópica como fuente histórica." *Gerión* 9:11–58.

———. 1992. "Lucha de clases e ideología: aproximación temática a las fábulas no contenidas en las colecciones anónimas." *Gerión* 10:23–63.

Castrucci, V. 1996. "Elementi orientali nella letteratura ellenistica: per una lettura di Callimacho, fr. 194 Pfeiffer." *Quaderni di Storia* 22, no. 43:279–293

Cavenaile, R., ed. 1958. *Corpus papyrorum Latinarum.* Wiesbaden: Otto Harrassowitz.

Chambry, E., ed. 1925. *Aesopi fabulae.* 2 vols. Paris: Société d'Édition "Les Belles Lettres." [Cf. review by Hausrath (1927).]

———, ed., trans. 1927. *Ésope: Fables.* Paris: Société d'Édition "Les Belles Lettres." [Cf. review by Hausrath (1927).]

Christes, J. 1979. "Reflexe erlebter Unfreiheit in den Sentenzen des Publilius Syrus und den Fabeln des Phaedrus: Zur Problematik ihrer Verifizierung." *Hermes* 107:199–220.

Cinquini, A. 1905. *Index Phaedrianus.* Milan. Reprint, Hildesheim: Olms, 1964.

Conybeare, F. C., J. R. Harris, and A. S. Lewis, eds. 1913. *The Story of Aḥiḳar: From the Aramaic, Syriac, Arabic, Armenian, Ethiopic, Old Turkish, Greek, and Slavonic Versions.* 2d ed. Cambridge.

Cozzoli, A.-T. 1995. "Poesia satirica latina e favola esopica (Ennio, Lucilio e Orazio)." *Rivista di Cultura Classica e Medioevale* 37:187–204.

Craven, T. C. 1973. "Studies in the Style of Phaedrus." Diss., McMaster University, Hamilton, Ontario.

Cremona, C. A. 1980. *Lexicon Phaedrianum.* Hildesheim and New York: Olms.

Crusius, O. 1879. "De Babrii aetate." [Diss., Leipzig.] *Leipziger Studien zur Classischen Philologie* 2:125–248.

———. 1894. "Fabeln des Babrius auf Wachstafeln aus Palmyra." *Philologus* 53:228–252.

———. 1896a. *Paulys Real-Encyclopädie der Classischen Altertumswissenschaft,* s.v. "Avianus." Stuttgart. 2:2373–2378.

———. 1896b. *Paulys Real-Encyclopädie der Classischen Altertumswissenschaft,* s.v. "Babrios." Stuttgart. 2:2655–2667.

————, ed. 1897. *Babrii fabulae Aesopeae. Accedunt fabularum dactylicarum et iambicarum reliquiae. Ignatii et aliorum tetrasticha iambica rec. a* C. F. Mueller. Leipzig: Teubner.

————. 1913. "Aus der Geschichte der Fabel." In *Das Buch der Fabeln,* edited by C. H. Kleukens, i–lxi. Reprint, Leipzig, 1920.

Currie, H. MacL. 1984. "Phaedrus the Fabulist." In *Aufstieg und Niedergang der Römischen Welt,* II 32, 1:497–513. Berlin: De Gruyter.

Dalfen, J. 1994–1995. "Die ὕβρις der Nachtigall: Zu der Fabel bei Hesiod (Erga 202–218) und zur griechischen Fabel im allgemeinen." *Wiener Studien* 107–108:157–177.

Daly, L. W., trans. 1961a. *Aesop without Morals: The Famous Fables, and a Life of Aesop.* New York and London: Yoseloff.

————. 1961b. "Hesiod's Fable." *Transactions and Proceedings of the American Philological Association* 92:45–51.

Dams, P. 1970. "Dichtungskritik bei nachaugusteischen Dichtern." Diss., Marburg. [Esp. 96–113: "Phaedrus."]

Davies, M. 1981. "Aeschylus and the Fable." *Hermes* 109:248–251.

————. 1987. "The Ancient Greeks on Why Mankind Does Not Live Forever." *Museum Helveticum* 44:65–75.

Degen, R. 1977. *Enzyklopädie des Märchens,* s.v. "Achikar." Berlin. 1:53–59.

Della Corte, F. 1966. "Tre papiri favolistici latini." In *Atti dell'XI Congresso Internazionale di Papirologia, Milano 2–8 settembre 1965,* 542–550. Milan. [= id. *Opuscula,* 4:147–155. Genoa: Università de Genova, Facolté di Lettere, 1973.]

————. 1986. "Orazio favolista." *Cultura e Scuola* 25:87–93. [= id. *Opuscula,* 11:35–41. Genoa: Università de Genova, Facolté di Lettere, 1988.]

Del Vecchio, L., and A. M. Fiore. 1998. "Fabula in satura: Osservazioni su alcuni frammenti delle Satire di Ennio." *Invigilata Lucernis* 20:59–72.

Desclos, M.-L. 1997. "'Le renard dit au lion . . . ' (Alcibiade Majeur, 123A), ou Socrate à la manière d'Ésope." In *L'animal dans l'antiquité,* edited by B. Cassin and J.-L. Labarrière, sous la direction de Gilbert Romeyer Dherbey, 395–422. Paris: Vrin.

Diels, H. 1910. "Orientalische Fabeln in griechischem Gewande." *Internationale Wochenschrift für Wissenschaft, Kunst und Technik* 4:993–1002.

Dijk, G.-J. van. 1993. "Theory and Terminology of the Greek Fable." *Reinardus* 6:171–183.

————. 1994a. Review of Holzberg 1992a. *Mnemosyne* 47:384–389.

————. 1994b. Review of Papathomopoulos 1989 and 1990. *Mnemosyne* 47:550–555.

————. 1995a. "'Εκ τῶν μύθων ἄρξασθαι. Greek Fable Theory after Aristotle: Characters and Characteristics." In *Greek Literary Theory after Aristotle: A Collection of Papers in Honour of D. M. Schenkeveld,* edited by J. G. J. Abbenes, S. R. Slings, and I. Sluiter, 235–258. Amsterdam: Vrije Universiteit Univ. Press.

————. 1995b. "The Fables in the Greek *Life of Aesop.*" *Reinardus* 8:131–150.

————. 1996. "The Function of Fables in Graeco-Roman Romance." *Mnemosyne* 49:513–541.

————. 1997. *ΑΙΝΟΙ, ΛΟΓΟΙ, ΜΥΘΟΙ: Fables in Archaic, Classical, and Hellenistic Greek Literature. With a Study of the Theory and Terminology of the Genre.* Mnemosyne, Supplement 166. Leiden, New York, and Cologne: Brill. [Cf. reviews by Gibbs (1998) and Holzberg (1998).]

Dillery, J. 1999. "Aesop, Isis, and the Heliconian Muses." *Classical Philology* 94:268–280.

Dimitriadou-Toufexi, E. 1981. "Index verborum Vitae Aesopi Perrianae." Ἐπιστημονικὴ ἐπετηρίδα τῆς φιλοσοφικῆς σχολῆς τοῦ Ἀριστοτελείου πανεπιστημίου Θεσσαλονίκης 20:69–153.

Draheim, H. 1889–1925. "Bericht über Litteratur zu Phaedrus und der römischen Fabeldichtung." *Jahresbericht über die Fortschritte der classischen Alterthumswissenschaft* 59:107–121; 68:210–225; 84: 235–258; 101:142–147; 126:149–158; 143:55–62; 183:195–203; 204:223–232.

Duff, J. W. 1927. *A Literary History of Rome in the Silver Age: From Tiberius to Hadrian.* London. [2d ed., 1960.] [107–127: "Phaedrus and Fable: Poetry of the Time."]

Duff, J. W. , and A. M. Duff, trans. 1934. *Minor Latin Poets.* Vol. 2. Loeb Classical Library. Cambridge, Mass., and London. [667–749: "Avianus."]

Eberhard, A., ed. 1872. *Fabulae Romanenses Graecae conscriptae.* Vol. 1, *De Syntipa et de Aesopo narrationes fabulosae partim ineditae.* Leipzig: Teubner.

Ellis, R., ed. 1887. *The Fables of Avianus.* Oxford. Reprint, Hildesheim: Olms, 1966.

Fales, F. M. 1993. "Storia di Ahiqar tra Oriente e Grecia: la prospettiva dall'antico Oriente." *Quaderni di Storia* 38:143–166.

Falkowitz, R. S. 1984. "Discrimination and Condensation of Sacred Categories." In *La fable: Huit exposés suivis de discussions,* edited by F. R. Adrados and O. Reverdin, 1–32. Entretiens sur l'Antiquité Classique, no. 30. Geneva: Fondation Hardt.

Fedeli, P. 1993. "La favola oraziana del topo di città e del topo di campagna: Una proposta di lettura." *Cultura e Scuola* 128: 42–52.

Ferrari, F. 1995a. "Per il testo della recensione G della Vita Aesopi." *Studi Classici e Orientali* 45:249–259.

———. 1995b. "*P. Oxy. 3331* e *Vita Aesopi* 18." *Zeitschrift für Papyrologie und Epigraphik* 107:296.

———, ed. 1997. *Romanzo di Esopo: Introduzione e testo critico . . . Traduzione e note di G. Bonelli e G. Sandrolini.* Milan: Classici della Biblioteca Universale Rizzoli.

Finch, Ch. E. 1971a. "The Morgan Manuscript of Phaedrus." *American Journal of Philology* 92:301–307.

———. 1971b. "Notes on the Fragment of Phaedrus in Reg. Lat. 1616." *Classical Philology* 66:190–191.

Fisher, B. F. 1987. "A History of the Use of Aesop's Fables as a School Text from the Classical Era through the Nineteenth Century." Ph.D. diss., Indiana University.

Foerster, R. 1895. "Lessing und Reiskes zu Aesop." *Rheinisches Museum* 50:66–89.

Fraenkel, E. 1924. "Zur Form der αἶνοι." *Rheinisches Museum* 73:366–370. [= id. *Kleine Beiträge zur Klassischen Philologie,* 1:235–239. Rome, 1964].

Gaide, F., ed. and trans. 1980. *Avianus: Fables.* Paris: Société d'Édition "Les Belles Lettres." [Cf. review by Küppers (1981).]

————. 1991. "Avianus, ses ambitions, ses résultats." In *La favolistica latina in distici elegiaci: Atti del Convegno Internazionale, Assisi, 26–28 ottobre 1990,* edited by G. Catanzaro and F. Santucci, 45–61. Assisi: Accademia Propertiana del Subasio, Centro Studi Poesia Latina in Distici Elegiaci.

Garcia, F. M., and A. R. Lopez. 1990. *Index mythiamborum Babrii.* Hildesheim, Zurich, and New York: Olms.

————. 1991. *Index Aesopi fabularum.* Hildesheim, Zurich, and New York: Olms.

Gatti, P. 1979. "Le favole del Monaco Ademaro e la tradizione manoscritta del corpus fedriano." *Sandalion* 2:247–256.

Getzlaff, E. 1907. "Quaestiones Babrianae et pseudo-Dositheanae." Diss., Marburg.

Giannattasio Andria, R. 1995. "Il *Bios* di Esopo e i primordi della biografia." In *Biografia e autobiografia degli antichi e dei moderni,* edited by I. Gallo and L. Nicastri, 41–56. Naples: Edizioni Scientifiche Italiane.

Gibbs, L. 1998. Review of van Dijk 1997. *Bryn Mawr Classical Review* 98.5.18.

Goetz, G., ed. 1892. *Hermeneumata Pseudodositheana.* Corpus Glossariorum Latinorum, vol. 3. Leipzig.

Gómez, P. 1990. "Αἶνος: el fill d'Isop." *Lexis* 5–6:81–88.

Grenfell, B. P., and A. S. Hunt, eds. 1897. *New Classical Fragments and Other Greek and Latin Papyri.* Greek Papyri, ser. 2. Oxford. [133–134: *PGrenfell II 84 = CFA* 1.2.119]

————, eds. 1901. *The Amherst Papyri.* Vol. 2, *Classical Fragments and Documents of the Ptolemaic, Roman, and Byzantine Periods.* London. [26–29: "XXVI. Babrius Fables."]

————. 1915. *The Oxyrhynchus Papyri: Part XI.* London. [247: 1404 = Cavenaile 1958, no. 38.]

Grubmüller, K. 1977. *Meister Esopus: Untersuchungen zu Geschichte und Funktion der Fabel im Mittelalter.* Münchener Texte und Untersuchungen zur Deutschen Literatur des Mittelalters, no. 56. Munich.

Guaglianone. A. 1956. "Gli 'Epimythia' di Aviano." *Atti dell'Accademia Pontaniana,* n.s., 5:353–377.

————. 1957. "La tradizione manoscritta di Aviano." *Rendiconti dell'Accademia di Archeologia, Lettere e Belle Arti,* n.s., 32:5–30.

————, ed. 1958. *Aviani Fabulae.* Corpus Scriptorum Latinorum Paravianum. Turin: Paravia.

————. 1968. "Fedro e il suo senario." *Rivista di Studi Classici* 16:91–104.

————, ed. 1969. *Phaedri Augusti liberti liber fabularum.* Turin: Paravia. [Cf. review by Nøjgaard (1972).]

Gual, C. G. 1977. "La fábula esópica: estructura e ideología de un género popular." In *Estudios ofrecidos a E. A. Llorach,* 1:309–322. Oviedo: Universidad de Oviedo.

Hägg, T. 1997. "A Professor and His Slave: Conventions and Values in the *Life of Aesop.*" In *Studies in Hellenistic Civilization VIII: Conventional Values of the Hellenistic Greeks,* edited by P. Bilde et al., 177–203. Aarhus: Aarhus University Press.

Halm, K., ed. 1852. *Fabulae Aesopicae collectae.* Leipzig: Teubner.

Handford, S. A. 1958–1961. Review of Hausrath 1940–1956. *The Journal of Hellenic Studies* 78:137–139; 81:174–175.

Hansen, W., ed. 1998. *Anthology of Ancient Greek Popular Literature.* Bloomington and Indianapolis: Indiana University Press.

Haslam, M. W. 1980–1986. *The Oxyrhynchus Papyri.* Vol. 47. London (53–56: "3331. Life of Aesop"). Part 53. London: British Academy. [149–172: "3720. Life of Aesop (Addendum to 3331)."].

———. 1992. Review of Papathomopoulos 1989 and 1990. *The Classical Review,* n.s., 42:188–189.

Hausrath, A. 1894. "Untersuchungen zur Überlieferung der äsopischen Fabeln." *Jahrbücher für classische Philologie,* Supplement 21:245–312.

———. 1898. "Das Problem der äsopischen Fabel." *Neue Jahrbücher für das classische Altertum* 1:305–322.

———. 1901. "Die Äsopstudien des Maximus Planudes." *Byzantinische Zeitschrift* 10:91–105.

———. 1909. *Paulys Real-Encyclopädie der Classischen Altertumswissenschaft,* s.v. "Fabel." Stuttgart. Vol. 6, no. 2, 1704–1736. [1707–1718: in *Fabelforschung,* ed. P. Hasubek, 38–52. Wege der Forschung 572. Darmstadt, 1983.]

———. 1910. Review of Thiele 1910. *Berliner philologische Wochenschrift* 30:1406–1413.

———. 1918. *Achiqar und Aesop: Das Verhältnis der orientalischen zur griechischen Fabeldichtung.* Sitzungsberichte der Heidelberger Akademie der Wissenschaften, Philosophisch-Historische Klasse, no. 2. Heidelberg.

———. 1927. Review of Chambry 1925 and 1927. *Philologische Wochenschrift* 47:1537–1546, 1569–1575.

———. 1936. "Zur Arbeitsweise des Phaedrus." *Hermes* 71:70–103.

———. 1937. Review of Perry 1936. *Philologische Wochenschrift* 57:770–777.

———. 1938. *Paulys Real-Encyclopädie der Classischen Altertumswissenschaft,* s.v. "Phaedrus." Stuttgart. Vol. 19, no. 2, 1475–1505.

———, ed. and trans. 1940. *Aesopische Fabeln. . . . Gefolgt von einer Abhandlung: Die Aesoplegende.* Munich: Heimeran.

———, ed. 1940–1956. *Corpus Fabularum Aesopicarum.* Vol. 1, *Fabulae Aesopicae soluta oratione conscriptae.* Fasc. 1 and 2. Leipzig: Teubner. [Fasc. 1:1970, Fasc. 2:1959 *curavit* H. Hunger; cf. reviews by Perry (1942), Adrados (1957), and Handford (1958–1961).]

Havas, L. 1989. "Fable and Historical Concept in Ancient Times." *Acta Antiqua Academiae Scientiarum Hungaricae* 32:63–73.

Heintze. H. von. 1989. "Das Grabrelief des Phaedrus." *Gymnasium* 96:1–12.

Henderson, J. 1999. "Phaedrus' Fables: The Original Corpus." *Mnemosyne* 52:308–329.

———. 2001. *Telling Tales on Caesar: Roman Stories from Phaedrus.* Oxford: Oxford University Press.

Hervieux, L. 1893–1894. *Les fabulistes latins depuis le siècle d'Auguste jusqu'à la fin du moyen âge.* 2 vols. Paris. Reprint, Hildesheim and New York: Olms, 1970.

Hesseling, D. C. 1892–1893. "On Waxen Tablets with Fables of Babrius (Tabulae ceratae Assendelftianae)." *The Journal of Hellenic Studies* 13:293–314.

Heydenreich, E. 1884–1888. "Bericht über die Litteratur zu Phädrus." *Jahresbericht über die Fortschritte der classischen Altertumswissenschaft* 39:1–33, 205–249; 43:100–124; 55:170–174.

Hillgruber, M. 1996. "Die Erzählung des Menenius Agrippa: Eine griechische Fabel in der römischen Geschichtsschreibung." *Antike und Abendland* 42:42–56.

Hilpert, R. 1992. "Bild und Text in Heinrich Steinhöwels 'leben des hochberühmten fabeldichters Esopi.'" In *Der Äsop-Roman: Motivgeschichte und Erzählstruktur,* edited by N. Holzberg, 131–154. Classica Monacensia, no. 6. Tübingen: Gunter Narr Verlag.

Hirsch, S. W. 1985–1986. "Cyrus' Parable of the Fish: Sea Power in the Early Relations of Greece and Persia." *The Classical Journal* 81: 222–229.

Hofmann, E. 1922. "Qua ratione ἔπος, μῦθος, αἶνος, λόγος et vocabula ab eisdem stirpibus derivata in antiquo Graecorum sermone (usque ad annum fere 400) adhibita sint." Diss., Göttingen.

Holbek, B. 1977. *Enzyklopädie des Märchens,* s.v., "Äsop." Berlin. 1:882–889.

Holzberg, N. 1991a. "Die Fabel von Stadtmaus und Landmaus bei Phaedrus und Horaz." *Würzburger Jahrbücher für die Altertumswissenschaft, n.s.,* 17:229–239.

———. 1991b. "Phaedrus in der Literaturkritik seit Lessing: Alte und neue Wege der Interpretation." *Anregung* 37:226–242.

———, ed. 1992a. *Der Äsop-Roman: Motivgeschichte und Erzählstruktur.* Classica Monacensia, no. 6. Tübingen: Gunter Narr Verlag.

———. 1992b. "Der Äsop-Roman: Eine strukturanalytische Interpretation." In *Der Äsop-Roman: Motivgeschichte und Erzählstruktur,* edited by N. Holzberg, 33–75. Classica Monacensia, no. 6. Tübingen: Gunter Narr Verlag.

———. 1993. "A Lesser-Known "Picaresque" Novel of Greek Origin: The *Aesop Romance* and Its Influence." In *Groningen Colloquia on the Novel,* no. 5, edited by H. Hofmann, 1–16. Groningen: Forsten.

———. 1996. "Fable: Aesop. Life of Aesop." In *The Novel in the Ancient World,* edited by G. Schmeling, 633–639. Mnemosyne, Supplement 159. Leiden, New York, and Cologne: Brill.

———. 1998. Review of van Dijk 1997. *Classical Review, n.s.,* 48:337–338.

———. 1999. "The Fabulist, the Scholars, and the Discourse: Aesop Studies Today." *International Journal of the Classical Tradition* 6:236–242.

Hopkins, K. 1993. "Novel Evidence for Roman Slavery." *Past & Present* 138:3–27.

Hostetter, W. H. 1955. "A Linguistic Study of the Vulgar Greek *Life of Aesop.*" Ph.D. diss., University of Illinois.

Hower, Ch. C. 1936. "Studies on the So-Called Accursiana Recension of the Life and Fables of Aesop." Ph.D. diss., University of Illinois.

Hubbard, T. K. 1995. "Hesiod's Fable of the Hawk and the Nightingale Reconsidered." *Greek, Roman and Byzantine Studies* 36:161–171.

Huber, G. 1990. *Das Motiv der "Witwe von Ephesus" in lateinischen Texten der Antike und des Mittelalters.* Mannheimer Beiträge zur Sprach- und Literaturwissenschaft, no. 18. Tübingen: Gunter Narr Verlag.

Husselmann, E. M. 1935. "A Lost Manuscript of the Fables of Babrius." *Transactions and Proceedings of the American Philological Association* 66:104–126.

Ihm, M. 1902. "Eine lateinische Babriosübersetzung." *Hermes* 37:147–151.

Immisch, O. 1930. "Babriana." *Rheinisches Museum* 79:153–169.

Irmscher, J., trans. 1978. *Antike Fabeln. Griechische Anfänge. Äsop. Fabeln in römischer Literatur. Phaedrus. Babrios. Romulus. Avian. Ignatios Diakonos.* Bibliothek der Antike. Berlin: Aufbau-Verlag. [3d ed., 1991]

Janko, R. 1980. "Aeschylus' *Oresteia* and Archilochus." *The Classical Quarterly,* n.s., 30:291–293.

Jedrkiewicz, S. 1987. "La favola esopica nel processo di argomentazione orale fino al IV sec. a. C." *Quaderni Urbinati di Cultura Classica* 56:35–63.

———. 1989. *Sapere e paradosso nell'antichità: Esopo e la favola.* Rome: Ateneo.

———. 1990. "Fedro e la verità." *Quaderni Urbinati di Cultura Classica* 63:121–128.

———. 1990–1992. "The Last Champion of Play-Wisdom: Aesop." *Itaca* 6–8:115–130.

———. 1994a. "La mujer del filósofo y la mulier de la filosofía." *Actas del IX Simposio de la Sociedad Española de Literatura General y Comparada.* Vol. 1, *La mujer: Elogio y vituperio,* 215–224. Saragossa: Universidad de Saragossa.

———. 1994b. "Quelques traits sceptiques dans l'image populaire du philosophe au début de notre ère." *Platon* 46:129–134.

———. 1997. *Il convitato sullo sgabello: Plutarco, Esopo ed i Setti Savi.* Pisa and Rome: Instituti Editoriali e Poligrafici Internazionali.

Jones, W. R. 1940. "The Text Tradition of Avianus." Ph.D. diss., University of Illinois.

———. 1969. "Avianus, Flavianus, Theodosius, and Macrobius." In *Classical Studies Presented to B. E. Perry,* 203–209. Urbana, Chicago, and London: University of Illinois Press.

Josifović, S. 1974. *Paulys Real-Encyclopädie der Classischen Altertumswissenschaft,* s.v. "Aisopos." Supplement 14:15–40.

Karadagli, T. 1981. *Fabel und Ainos: Studien zur griechischen Fabel.* Beiträge zur Klassischen Philologie, no. 135. Königstein im Taunus: Anton Hain.

Knöll, P., ed. 1877. *Fabularum Babrianarum paraphrasis Bodleiana.* Vienna.

Koep, L. 1969. *Reallexikon für Antike und Christentum,* s.v. "Fabel." Stuttgart. 7:129–154.

Korzeniewski, D. 1970. "Zur Verstechnik des Phaedrus: Aufgelöste Hebungen und Senkungen in seinen Senaren." *Hermes* 98:430–458.

Koster, S. 1991. "Phaedrus: Skizze einer Selbstauffassung." In *Die Antike im Brennpunkt,* edited by P. Neukam, 59–87. Dialog Schule-Wissenschaft. Klassische Sprachen und Literaturen , no. 25. Munich: Bayerischer Schulbuch-Verlag.

Kramer, B., and D. Hagedorn, eds. 1978. *Kölner Papyri (P.Köln).* Vol. 2. Opladen: Westdeutscher-Verlag. [56–61: "Zwei Fabeln."]

Küppers, J. 1977. *Die Fabeln Avians: Studien zur Darstellung und Erzählweise spätantiker Fabeldichtung.* Habelts Dissertationsdrucke. Reihe Klassische Philologie, vol. 26. Bonn: Habelt.

———. 1981. Review of Gaide 1980. *Gnomon* 53:239–245.

————. 1990. "Zu Eigenart und Rezeptionsgeschichte der antiken Fabeldichtung." In *Arbor amoena comis: 25 Jahre Mittellateinisches Seminar in Bonn, 1965–1990,* edited by E. Könsgen, 23–33. Stuttgart: Franz Steiner.

Kussl, R. 1992. "Achikar, Tinuphis und Äsop." In *Der Äsop-Roman: Motivgeschichte und Erzählstruktur,* edited by N. Holzberg, 23–30. Classica Monacensia, no. 6. Tübingen: Gunter Narr Verlag.

Lamb, R. W. 1998. *Annales Phaedriani, 1596–1996.* Lowestoft: privately printed.

Lamberti, G. 1980. "La poetica del *lusus* in Fedro." *Rendiconti Istituto Lombardo, Classe di Lettere e Scienze Morali e Storiche* 114:95–115.

La Penna, A. 1961. "La morale della favola esopica come morale delle classe subalterne nell'antichità." *Società* 17:459–537.

————. 1962. "Il romanzo di Esopo." *Athenaeum,* n.s., 40:264–314.

————. 1964. "Letteratura esopica e letteratura assiro-babilonese." *Rivista di Filologia e di Istruzione Classica* 92:24–39.

————. 1966. Review of Nøjgaard 1964–1967. *Athenaeum,* n.s., 44:354–369.

————. 1997. "Una favola esopica e l'interpretazione di Catullo 96." *Studi Italiani di Filologia Classica,* 3d ser., 15:246–249.

Lasserre, F. 1984. "La fable en Grèce dans la poésie archaïque." In *La fable: Huit exposés suivis de discussions,* edited by F. R. Adrados and O. Reverdin, 61–103. Entretiens sur l'Antiquité Classique, no. 30. Geneva: Fondation Hardt.

Leclerc, M.-C. 1992. "L'épervier et le rossignol d'Hésiode: Une fable à double sens." *Revue des Études Grecques* 105:37–44.

Lindenberger, J. M., trans. 1985. "Ahiqar: A New Translation and Introduction." In *The Old Testament Pseudepigrapha,* edited by J. H. Charlesworth, 2:479–507. London: Darton, Longman and Todd.

Livrea, E. 1970. "L'αἶνος esiodeo." *Giornale Italiano di Filologia* 22, no. 2:1–20.

Lonsdale, S. H. 1989. "Hesiod's Hawk and Nightingale (Op. 202–12): Fable or Omen?" *Hermes* 117: 403–412.

Lorenzi, A. de. 1955. *Fedro.* Florence: La Nuova Italia Editrice.

Ludwig, C. 1997. *Sonderformen byzantinischer Hagiographie und ihr literarisches Vorbild: Untersuchungen zu den Viten des Äsop, des Philaretos, des Symeon Salos und des Andreas Salos.* Berliner Byzantinische Studien 3. Frankfurt am Main, Bern, New York, and Paris: Peter Lang.

Luzzatto, M. J. 1975. "La cultura letteraria di Babrio." *Annali della Scuola Normale Superiore di Pisa: Classe di lettere e filosofia,* 3d ser., 5, no. 1:17–97.

————, ed. 1976. *Fedro. Un poeta tra favola e realtà: Antologia. Con un saggio di L. Mondo.* Turin: Paravia.

————. 1979. Review of Pisi 1977. *Atene e Roma,* n.s., 24:187–190.

————. 1983. "La datazione della Collectio Augustana di Esopo ed il verso politico delle origini." *Jahrbuch der Österreichischen Byzantinistik* 33:137–177.

————. 1984. "Note su Aviano e sulle raccolte esopiche greco-latine." *Prometheus* 10:75–94.

————. 1985. "Fra poesia e retorica: la clausola del 'coliambo' di Babrio." *Quaderni Urbinati di Cultura Classica* 48:97–127.

————. 1988. "Plutarco, Socrate e l'Esopo di Delfi." *Illinois Classical Studies* 13:427–445.

————. 1992. "Grecia e vicino oriente: tracce della 'Storia di Ahiqar' nella cultura greca tra VI e V secolo a. C." *Quaderni di Storia* 36:5–84.

————. 1994. "Ancora sulla 'Storia di Ahiqar.'" *Quaderni di Storia* 39: 253–277.

————. 1996a. *Der Neue Pauly,* s.v. "Aisopos." Stuttgart. 1:360–365.

————. 1996b. *Der Neue Pauly,* s.v. "Aisop-Roman." Stuttgart. 1:359–360.

————. 1996c. "Esopo." In *I greci: storia cultura arte società* 2, no.1, edited by S. Setti, 1307–1324. Turin: Einaudi.

————, and A. La Penna, eds. 1986. *Babrii Mythiambi Aesopei.* Leipzig: Teubner.

Marc, P. 1910. "Die Überlieferung des Äsopromans." *Byzantinische Zeitschrift* 19:383–421.

Maria, L. de. 1987. *La femina in Fedro. Emarginazione e privilegio.* Lecce: Adriatici Editrice.

Marinčič, M. 1995. "Die Symbolik im Buch Tobit und der Achikar-Roman." *Živa Antika* 45:199–212.

Marrou, H.-I. 1957. *Geschichte der Erziehung im klassischen Altertum.* Freiburg and Munich: Alber.

Massarro, M. 1979. "*Variatio* e sinonimia in Fedro." *Invigilata Lucernis* 1:89–142.

————. 1981a. "La redazione fedriana della 'Matrona di Efeso.'" *Materiali e contributi per la storia della narrativa greco-latina* 3:217–237.

————. 1981b. "Una caratteristica dello stile di Fedro: La *variato sermonis*." *Quaderni dell'Associazione italiana di cultura classica* 1:49–61.

Menna, F. 1983. "La ricerca dell'adiuvante: sulla favoletta esopica dell'allodola (Enn. Sat. 21–58 Vahl.²; Babr. 88; Avian. 21)." *Materiali e discussioni per l'analisi dei testi classici* 10–11:105–132.

Merkle, S. 1992. "Die Fabel von Frosch und Maus: Zur Funktion der λόγοι im Delphi-Teil des Äsop-Romans." In *Der Äsop-Roman: Motivgeschichte und Erzählstruktur,* edited by N. Holzberg, 110–127. Classica Monacensia, no. 6. Tübingen: Gunter Narr Verlag.

————. 1996. "Fable, 'anecdote' and 'novella' in the Vita Aesopi: The ingredients of a 'popular novel.'" In *La letteratura di consumo nel mondo greco-latino,* edited by O. Pecere and A. Stramaglia, 209–234. Cassino: Università degli Studi di Cassino.

Meuli, K. 1954. "Herkunft und Wesen der Fabel." *Schweizerisches Archiv für Volkskunde* 50:65–88. [= id. *Gesammelte Schriften,* 2:731–756. Basel and Stuttgart: Schwabe, 1975; cf. review by Perry (1957)].

Meyer, E. 1912. *Der Papyrusfund von Elephantine.* Leipzig.

Mignogna, E. 1992. "Aesopus bucolicus: Come si 'mette in scena' un miraculo (Vita Aesopi c. 6)." In *Der Äsop-Roman: Motivgeschichte und Erzählstruktur,* edited by N. Holzberg, 76–84. Classica Monacensia, no. 6. Tübingen: Gunter Narr Verlag.

Möllendorff, P. von. 1994. "Die Fabel von Adler und Mistkäfer im Äsop-roman." *Rheinisches Museum* 137:141–161.

Moretti, G. 1982. "Lessico giuridico e modello giudiziario nella favola fedriana." *Maia,* n.s., 34:227–240.

Müller, C. W. 1976. "Ennius und Äsop." *Museum Helveticum* 33:193–218.

————. 1980. "Die Witwe von Ephesus—Petrons Novelle und die 'Milesiaka' des Aristeides." *Antike und Abendland* 26:103–121.

Nappa, C. 1994. "Agamemnon 717–36: The Parable of the Lion Cub." *Mnemosyne* 47:82–87.

Narkiss, D. 1995. "Beginning Again: On Aristotle's Use of a Fable in the *Meteorologica*." *Scripta Classica Israelica* 14:42–51.

Nøjgaard, M. 1964–1967. *La fable antique*. Vol. 1, *La fable grecque avant Phèdre*. Vol. 2, *Les grands fabulistes*. Copenhagen: Nyt Nordisk Forlag, Arnold Busck. [Cf. reviews by Adrados (1965–1970) and La Penna (1966).]

————. 1972. Review of Guaglianone 1969. *Gnomon* 44:569–575.

————. 1979. "The Moralisation of the Fable: From Æsop to Romulus." In *Medieval Narrative: A Symposium. Proceedings of the Third International Symposium Organized by the Centre for the Study of Vernacular Literature in the Middle Ages*, edited by H. Bekker-Nielsen, 31–43. Odense: Odense University Press.

————. 1984. "La moralisation de la fable: D'Ésope à Romulus." In *La fable: Huit exposés suivis de discussions*, edited by F. R. Adrados and O. Reverdin, 225–251. Entretiens sur l'Antiquité Classique, no. 30. Geneva: Fondation Hardt.

————. 1986. Review of Adrados 1979–1987. *Gnomon* 58:193–198.

Oberg, E., ed. and trans. 1996a. *Phaedrus, Fabeln*. Sammlung Tusculum. Zurich and Düsseldorf: Artemis.

————. 1996b. "Römische Rechtspflege bei Phaedrus." *Rheinisches Museum* 139:146–165.

————. 1997. "*Mulier mala dicendi perita*—Die Frauen bei Phaedrus." In *Vir bonus dicendi peritus. Festschrift für A. Weische zum 65. Geburtstag*, edited by B. Czapla, T. Lehmann, and S. Liell, 311–320. Wiesbaden: Reichert.

————. 1999. "Frauen und andere 'Merkwürdigkeiten': Sokratische Züge in den Fabeln des Phaedrus." In *Das Lächeln des Sokrates*, edited by H. Kessler, 103–128. Sokrates-Studien, no. 4. Kusterdingen: Servicecenter Fachverlag GmbH.

————. 2000. *Phaedrus-Kommentar*. Stuttgart: Franz Steiner.

Önnerfors, A. 1987. "Textkritisches und Sprachliches zu Phaedrus." *Hermes* 115:429–452.

Oettinger, N. 1992. "Achikars Weisheitssprüche im Licht älterer Fabeldichtung." In *Der Äsop-Roman: Motivgeschichte und Erzählstruktur*, edited by N. Holzberg, 3–22. Classica Monacensia, no. 6. Tübingen: Gunter Narr Verlag.

Oldfather, W. A. 1929. "An Aesopic Fable in a Schoolboy's Exercise." *Aegyptus* 10:255–256.

————. 1940. Review of Roberts 1938. *American Journal of Philology* 61:211–221 [216–218: B. E. Perry on *Papyrus Rylands 493*].

Olshausen, E. 1995. "Der Bürgerkrieg und die Betroffenheit des einfachen Mannes: Eine Interpretation der Phaedrus-Fabel vom alten Mann und dem Eselchen (Phaedrus 1, 15/16 B.)." In *Historische Interpretationen. Gerold Walser zum 75. Geburtstag dargebracht von Freunden, Kollegen und Schülern*, edited by M. Weinmann-Walser, 123–130. Historia Einzelschriften, no. 100. Stuttgart: Franz Steiner.

Papademetriou, J.-Th. 1997. *Aesop as an Archetypal Hero*. Studies and Researches, no. 39. Athens: Hellenic Society for Humanistic Studies. [Cf. review by Holzberg (1999).]

Papathomopoulos, M. 1989. *Aesopus revisitatus: Recherches sur le texte des Vies Ésopiques*. Vol. 1, *La critique textuelle*. Joannina: Panepistemio Ioanninon, Philosophike Schole. [Cf. review by Haslam (1992).]

———, ed. and trans. 1991. Ὁ Βίος τοῦ Αἰσώπου. Ἡ Παραλλαγὴ G. Κριτικὴ ἔκδοση μὲ εἰσαγωγὴ καὶ μετάφραση. 2d ed. Joannina: Joannina University Press. [Cf. review by Haslam (1992).]

———, ed. and trans. 1999a. Ὁ Βίος τοῦ Αἰσώπου. Ἡ Παραλλαγή W. Editio princeps. Εἰσαγωγή — Κείμενο — Μετάφραση — Σχόλια. Athens: Εκδοσεις Παναδήμα.

———, ed. 1999b. Πέντε δημώδεις μετάφρασεις τοῦ Βίου τοῦ Αἰσώπου. Athens: Εκδοσεις Παναδήμα.

Patterson, A. 1991. *Fables of Power: Aesopian Writing and Political History*. Durham and London: Duke University Press.

Paulis, G. de. 1997. *Aviani index et lexicon*. Alpha-Omega. Reihe A, Lexika, Indizes, Konkordanzen zur klassischen Philologie, no. 184. Hildesheim: Olms.

Peil, D. 1985. *Der Streit der Glieder mit dem Magen: Studien zur Überlieferungs- und Deutungsgeschichte der Fabel des Menenius Agrippa von der Antike bis ins 20. Jahrhundert*. Mikrokosmos, no. 16. Frankfurt am Main, Bern, and New York: Peter Lang.

Perry, B. E. 1933. "The Text Tradition of the Greek Life of Aesop." *Transactions and Proceedings of the American Philological Association* 64: 198–244.

———. 1936. *Studies in the Text History of the Life and Fables of Aesop*. Haverford: American Philological Association. [Cf. review by Hausrath (1937).]

———. 1940. "The Origin of the Epimythium." *Transactions and Proceedings of the American Philological Association* 71:391–419.

———. 1942. Review of Hausrath 1940–1956. *Classical Philology* 37: 207–218.

———, ed. 1952. *Aesopica: A Series of Texts Relating to Aesop or Ascribed to Him or Closely Connected with the Literary Tradition That Bears His Name. Collected and Critically Edited, in Part Translated from Oriental Languages, with a Commentary and Historical Essay*. Vol. 1, *Greek and Latin Texts*. Urbana: University of Illinois Press. Reprint, New York: Arno Press, 1980. [Cf. review by Adrados (1953).]

———. 1953. "An Aesopic Fable in Photius." *Byzantinische Zeitschrift* 46: 308–313.

———. 1957. Review of Meuli 1954. *Gnomon* 29:427–431.

———. 1959. "Fable." *Studium Generale* 12:17–37.

———. 1962. "Demetrius of Phalerum and the Aesopic Fables." *Transactions and Proceedings of the American Philological Association* 93:287–346.

———, trans. 1965. *Babrius and Phaedrus*. Loeb Classical Library. Cambridge and London: Harvard University Press.

———. 1966. "Some Addenda to the Life of Aesop." *Byzantinische Zeitschrift* 59:285–304.

Pervo, R. 1998. "A Nihilist Fabula: Introducing *The Life of Aesop.*" In *Ancient Fiction and Early Christian Narrative,* edited by R. F. Hock, J. B. Chance, and J. Perkins, 77–120. Society of Biblical Literature, Symposium Series 6. Atlanta: Scholars Press.

Pesce, M., and A. Destro. 1999. "La lavanda dei piedi di Gv 13, 1–20, il *Romanzo di Esopo* e i *Saturnalia* di Macrobio." *Biblica* 80:240–249.

Pillolla, M. P. 1991. "Reminiscenze e aggettivazione allusiva in due favole di Aviano." In *La favolistica latina in distici elegiaci: Atti del Convegno Internazionale, Assisi, 26–28 ottobre 1990,* edited by G. Catanzaro and F. Santucci, 215–223. Assisi: Accademia Propertiana del Subasio, Centro Studi Poesia Latina in Distici Elegiaci.

——. 1994. "Plauto in Esopo (Echi comici in una traduzione quattrocentesca)." *Maia* 46:301–313.

Pisi, G. 1977. *Fedro traduttore di Esopo.* Florence: La Nuova Italia Editrice. [Cf. review by Luzzatto (1979).]

Poethke, G., trans. 1974. *Das Leben Äsops. Mit Einleitung herausgegeben und erläutert von W. Müller.* Leipzig: Dieterich'sche Verlagsbuchhandlung.

Port, W. 1933–1939. "Die Literatur zur griechischen und römischen Fabel." *Jahresbericht über die Fortschritte der klassischen Altertumswissenschaft* 240:63–94; 265:1–29.

Pugliarello, M. 1981–1982. "Appunti di sintassi fedriana." *Studi e Ricerche dell'Istituto di Latino* 4:109–121; 5:101–117.

Radermacher. L. 1902. "Aus dem zweiten Bande der Amherst Papyri." *Rheinisches Museum* 57:137–151. [142–145: on *P.Amherst II.26*].

Ragone, G. 1997. "La schiavità di Esopo a Samo: Storia e romanzo." In *Schiavi e dipendenti nell'ambito dell"oikos' e della 'familia': Atti del XXII Colloquio GIREA Pontignano (Siena) 19–20 novembre 1995,* edited by M. Moggi and G. Cordiano, 127–171. Pisa: Edizioni ETS.

Riedel, V., ed. and trans. 1989. *Phaedrus: Der Wolf und das Lamm. Fabeln.* Leipzig: Reclam.

Robert, U., ed. 1893. *Les fables de Phèdre: Édition paléographique publiée d'après le manuscrit Rosanbo.* Paris.

Roberts, C. H. 1938. *Catalogue of the Greek and Latin Papyri in the John Rylands Library, Manchester.* Vol. 3, *Theological and Literary Texts (nos. 457–551).* Manchester: Manchester University Press. [119–128: "493. Aesop (?), Fables."; cf. Perry in Oldfather 1940.]

——. 1957. "A Fable Recovered." *The Journal of Roman Studies* 47: 124–125.

Rothwell, Jr., K. S. 1995. "Aristophanes' *Wasps* and the Sociopolitics of Aesop's Fables." *The Classical Journal* 90:233–254.

Rutherford, W. G., ed. 1883. *Babrius, ed. with Introductory Dissertations, Critical Notes, Commentary and Lexicon.* London.

Sanders, H. A. 1947. *Latin papyri in the University of Michigan Collection.* Michigan Papyri, no. 7. Ann Arbor: University of Michigan Press. [No. 457 ~ *Aes.* 39.]

Sbordone, F. 1932. "Recensioni retoriche delle favole esopiane." *Rivista Indo-Greca-Italica di Filologia* 16:35–68.

Schanz, M., and C. Hosius. 1935. *Geschichte der römischen Literatur.* Vol. 2, no. 4. Munich. [447–456: "Phaedrus."]

Schauer, M., and S. Merkle. 1992. "Äsop und Sokrates." In *Der Äsop-Roman: Motivgeschichte und Erzählstruktur,* edited by N. Holzberg, 85–96. Classica Monacensia, no. 6. Tübingen: Gunter Narr Verlag.

Schmidt, P. L. 1979. "Politisches Argument und moralischer Appell: Zur Historizität der antiken Fabel im frühkaiserzeitlichen Rom." *Der Deutschunterricht* 31, no. 6:74–88.

Shiner, W. 1998. "Creating Plot in Episodic Narratives: The *Life of Aesop* and the Gospel of Mark." In *Ancient Fiction and Early Christian Narrative,* edited by R. F. Hock, J. B. Chance, and J. Perkins, 155–176. Society of Biblical Literature, Symposium Series 6. Atlanta: Scholars Press.

Sitzler, J. 1897–1922. "Bericht über die griechischen Lyriker." *Jahresbericht über die Fortschritte der classischen Altertumswissenschaft* 92:1–204. [Babrius: 109–115]; 104:76–164 [Babrius: 104–106]; 133:104–322 [Babrius: 162–165]; 191:27–77 [Babrius: 51].

Smend, R. 1908. "Alter und Herkunft des Achikar-Romans und sein Verhältnis zu Aesop." In *Beiträge zur Erklärung und Kritik des Buches Tobit / R. S.,* edited by J. Müller, 55–125. Beihefte zur Zeitschrift für die alttestamentliche Wissenschaft, Gießen.

Speckenbach, K. 1978. "Die Fabel von der Fabel: Zur Überlieferungsgeschichte der Fabel von Hahn und Perle." *Frühmittelalterliche Studien* 12:178–229.

Spoerri, Th. 1942–1943. "Der Aufstand der Fabel." *Trivium* 1:31–63. [Also in *Fabelforschung,* edited by P. Hasubek, 97–127. Wege der Forschung 572. Darmstadt.]

Tartuferi, P. 1984. "Phaedr. I 5 [vacca, capella, ovis et leo]: Nota su Fedro e la tradizione esopica." *Annali della Facoltà di Lettere e Filosofia, Università di Macerata* 17:321–333.

Temple, O., and R. Temple, trans. 1998. *Aesop: The Complete Fables.* London: Penguin Classics.

Thiele, G., ed. 1905. *Der illustrierte lateinische Äsop in der Handschrift des Ademar: Codex Vossianus Lat. oct. 15, fol. 195–205.* Leiden.

———. 1906–1911. "Phaedrus-Studien." *Hermes* 41:562–592; 43:337–372; 46:376–392.

———. 1908. "Die vorliterarische Fabel der Griechen." *Neue Jahrbücher für das klassische Altertum* 21:377–400.

———, ed. 1910. *Der Lateinische Äsop des Romulus und die Prosa-Fassungen des Phädrus.* Heidelberg. Reprint, Hildesheim, Zurich, and New York: Olms, 1985. [Cf. review by Hausrath (1910).]

Thraede, K. 1968–1969. "Zu Ausonius ep. 16,2 (Sch.)." *Hermes* 96:608–628.

Tortora, L. 1975. "Recenti studi su Fedro (1967–1974)." *Bollettino di studi latini* 5:266–273.

Unrein, O. 1885. "De Aviani aetate." Diss., Jena.

Vaio, J. 1970. "An Alleged Paraphrase of Babrius." *Greek, Roman and Byzantine Studies* 11:49–52.

———. 1977. "A New Manuscript of Babrius: Fact or Fable?" *Illinois Classical Studies* 2:173–183.

———. 1980. "New Non-Evidence for the Name of Babrius." *Emérita* 48:1–3.

————. 1981. "Another Forgery from the Pen of Mynas? (Paris suppl. gr. 1245)." In *Corolla Londiniensis*, edited by G. Giangrande, 113–127. London Studies in Classical Philology, no. 8. Amsterdam: Gieben.

————. 1984. "Babrius and the Byzantine Fable." In *La fable: Huit exposés suivis de discussions*, edited by F. R. Adrados and O. Reverdin, 197–224. Entretiens sur l'Antiquité Classique, no. 30. Geneva: Fondation Hardt.

————. 1994. "Babrius, Fab. 78: A New MS." *Illinois Classical Studies* 19:205–208.

Wagner, F. 1977. *Enzyklopädie des Märchens*, s.v. "Babrios." Berlin. 1:1123–1128.

Warmuth, G. 1992. *Autobiographische Tierbilder bei Horaz*. Altertumswissenschaftliche Texte und Studien, no. 22. Hildesheim, Zurich, and New York: Olms.

Wehrli, F. 1949. *Die Schule des Aristoteles: Texte und Kommentare*. Vol. 4, *Demetrios von Phaleron*. Basel: Schwabe.

Weinreich, O. 1931. *Fabel, Aretalogie, Novelle: Beiträge zu Phädrus, Petron, Martial und Apuleius*. Sitzungsberichte der Heidelberger Akademie der Wissenschaften, Philosoph.-Hist. Klasse, no. 7. Heidelberg: Winter.

West, M. L. 1974. *Studies in Greek Elegy and Iambus*. Berlin and New York: De Gruyter.

————, ed. 1978. *Hesiod: Works & Days*. Oxford: Clarendon Press.

————. 1979. "The Parodos of the *Agamemnon*." *The Classical Quarterly*, n.s., 29:1–6.

————. 1982. "Archilochus' Fox and Eagle: More Echoes in Later Poetry." *Zeitschrift für Papyrologie und Epigraphik* 45:30–32.

————. 1984. "The Ascription of Fables to Aesop in Archaic and Classical Greece." In *La fable: Huit exposés suivis de discussions*, edited by F. R. Adrados and O. Reverdin, 105–136. Entretiens sur l'Antiquité Classique, no. 30. Geneva: Fondation Hardt.

Westermann, A., ed. 1845. *Vita Aesopi: Ex Vratislaviensi ac partim Monacensi et Vindobonensi codicibus*. Brunswick and London.

Wiechers, A. 1961. *Aesop in Delphi*. Beiträge zur Klassische Philologie, no. 2. Meisenheim am Glann: Hain.

Wienert, W. 1925. *Die Typen der griechisch-römischen Fabel*. Helsinki.

Wills, L. M. 1997. *The Quest of the Historical Gospel. Mark, John, and the Origin of the Gospel Genre*. London and New York: Routledge.

Wilsdorf, H. 1991. "Der weise Achikaros bei Demokrit und Theophrast: Eine Kommunikationsfrage." *Philologus* 135:191–206.

Winkler, J. J. 1985. *Auctor & Actor: A Narratological Reading of Apuleius's "The Golden Ass."* Berkeley, Los Angeles, and London: University of California Press. [276–291: "Isis and Aesop."]

Wissemann, M. 1992. "Fabel: Zur Entwicklung der Bezeichnung für eine Literaturgattung." *Fabula* 33:1–13.

Wright, A. T. 1997. "Iste auctor ab aliis differt: Avianus and his medieval readers." In *Fremdes wahrnehmen—fremdes Wahrnehmen*, edited by W. Harms and C. S. Jaeger, 9–19. Stuttgart and Leipzig: Hirzel.

Zafiropoulos, C. A. 2001. *Ethics in Aesop's Fables: The "Augustana Collection."* Mnemosyne, Supplement 216. Leiden, Boston, and Cologne: Brill.

Zander, C. M. 1897. *De generibus et libris paraphrasium Phaedrianarum.* Lund.

———. 1921. *Phaedrus solutus vel Phaedri fabulae novae XXX: Quas fabulas prosarias Phaedro vindicavit recensuit metrumque restituit.* Lund.

Zeitz, H. 1935. *Die Fragmente des Äsopromans in Papyrushandschriften.* Diss., Gießen.

———. 1936. "Der Aesoproman und seine Geschichte: Eine Untersuchung im Anschluß an die neugefundenen Papyri." *Aegyptus* 16:225–256.

Zimmermann, R. Ch. W. 1933. "Die Zeit des Babrios." *Bayerische Blätter für das Gymnasial-Schulwesen* 69:310–318.

Zinato, A. 1989. "'Possibile' e 'impossibile' nella favola esopica." In *Il meraviglioso e il verosimile tra antichità e medioevo,* edited by D. Lanza and O. Longo, 239–248. Florence: Olscki.

Zwierlein, O. 1970. "Der Codex Pithoeanus des Phaedrus in der Pierpont Morgan Library." *Rheinisches Museum* 113:91–93.

———. 1989. "Jupiter und die Frösche." *Hermes* 117:182–191.

GENERAL INDEX

Accursius, Bonus, 73
Ademar of Chabannes, 4, 40, 96
Aeschylus, 12, 13, 18, 19, 20, 36
Aesop, 11, 15f., 19, 26, 27, 29, 36, 45, 63, 74, 77f., 81, 88, 91, 95
Aesop Romance, 3, 76–84
  and the *Ahikar Romance,* 78, 81, 84, 93
  appearances and reality, 27, 83f.
  authentication, 74
  author, 74–76, 84f., 91, 92
  Codex Cryptoferratensis, 6, 72f.
  and the *Collectio Augustana,* 72–76, 84f., 90f., 91f.
  and contemporary cults, 94
  contents, 77f.
  date, 75
  fable structure, 90f.
  genesis, 77, 78, 93
  and the Gospels, 94
  inserted fables, 75, 79–81
  Nachleben, 94
  narrative structure, 78–84, 90f., 94
  socio-historical interpretation, 94
  sources, 78f., 93
  textual history, 72–74, 93
  Vita G, 72, 73, 74, 76, 93
  Vita Pl, 73, 74, 76, 93
  Vita W, 73, 74, 76, 93
Aesopus Latinus, 3, 4, 40, 95–104
  Ademar Codex, 3, 4, 40, 50, 96, 104
  authentication, 95, 98
  author's intention, 102–104

book structure, 98f.
date, 98
genesis, 102
language and style, 100f.
narrative technique, 103
and Phaedrus, 95f., 98, 100–102, 103
promythia and *epimythia,* 101
relationship between the four *recensiones,* 98f., 103f.
"Romulus," 4, 95–97, 98, 99, 102, 103
sources, 95f.
textual history, 98, 104
Wissembourg Codex, 4, 97–99
Ahikar Romance, 14, 15, 78, 79, 80, 81, 84, 93
Anthologia Palatina, 58, 63
Aphthonius, 2, 20, 29, 31, 38, 58
Appianus, 17
Apuleius, 28, 32, 76
Archilochus, 12, 14, 18, 33, 36, 52
Aristides, Aelius, 26
Aristophanes, 12, 13, 15, 16, 18, 19, 20, 21, 29, 36
Aristotle, 11f., 13, 17, 19, 20, 23, 24, 34, 36
Avianus, 1, 3, 58, 62–71
  book structure, 65, 70, 99
  date, 68f., 70
  intention, 69
  meter, 63, 66f.
  Nachleben, 70, 71
  narrative technique, 63, 66–68
  and Phaedrus, 63, 64, 65

Avianus (*continued*)
  sources, 64f., 70
  textual history, 70
  and Virgil, 67, 68

Babrius, 3, 52–62
  book structure, 53–55, 85
  Codex Athous, 3, 53, 54, 55, 65
  and the *Collectio Augustana,* 59
  date, 59
  epimythia, 57f., 60, 61
  language and style, 58, 60
  lion fables, 54, 61
  Nachleben, 30, 64f.
  narrative technique, 56f.
  politics, 60f.
  prose paraphrases, 3, 53, 54, 62
  sources, 58–60
  tetrasticha, 58, 63
  textual history, 53
Batrachomyomachia, 18

Callimachus, 18, 19, 22, 36, 52, 53
Catullus, 32, 38
Chambry, E., 5, 6, 7, 62
Collectio Accursiana, 4, 6, 73f.
Collectio Augustana, 4, 5f., 73f.,
    84–95
  and the *Aesop Romance,* 72–76,
    84f., 90f., 91f.
  appearances and reality, 27f., 91f.
  author, 74–76, 84f., 87f., 91, 92
  and Babrius, 88
  book structure, 53f. 85
  Codex Monacensis gr. 564, 4, 7, 73
  date, 75, 94
  epimythia, 88f.
  ethical content, 95
  fables ending in lament, 87, 90f.
  formulaic language, 20, 21,
    87–89, 90
  humor, 90
  language and style, 75, 87f.
  narrative technique, 86–88
  sources, 88, 89
  textual history, 73f., 94

Collectio Vindobonensis, 4, 6, 73f.
Crusius, O., 8, 10

Demetrius of Phalerum, 11, 22–25,
    37
Dio of Prusa, 25, 26
Diodorus, 17
Diogenes Laertius, 22
Diogenes of Sinope, 26, 79
Dionysius of Halicarnassus, 17

Ennius, 18, 32, 33, 38, 59
Eulenspiegel, Till, 76, 80

Fable
  conformist ideology, 49, 61
  definition of the genre, 8, 11, 19,
    36f., 68
  as exemplum, 2, 11–38
  formulaic language, 20f., 24, 33,
    35, 37
  history of collections, 5, 94
  Mesopotamian influences,
    13–15, 16, 19, 36, 60, 85
  moral satire, 18, 27–29
  narrative structure, 20f.
  philosophical exemplum, 17f.
  promptuarium, 23–25, 45
  promythium, 24, 44f.
  use in schools, 2, 29–31, 37f.
  socio-historical interpretation, 8,
    16, 36, 46f.
  scholarship, 1–10, 35–38, 50–52,
    62, 70f., 93–95, 104
  types
    aition, 19, 87
    'vying-match,' 19, 87
Fronto, 32

Gellius, 33, 59
Gregory of Nyssa, 28
Grubmüller, K., 8, 103

Halm, K., 7
Hausrath, A., 6
Hermogenes, 29

Herodotus, 2, 12, 15, 17, 36
Hesiod, 12, 13, 14, 16, 17, 21, 36, 79
Himerius, 26
Horace, 18, 32, 34f., 38, 41f., 47f., 63

Ibycus, 13, 17, 19
Ignatius Diaconus, 90

Josephus, Flavius, 17, 59

Lessing, G. E., 7, 76
Libanius, 26
Livy, 17, 31f., 38
Lucian, 18, 27–29, 92. *See also* Ps.-Lucian, *Lucius, or The Ass*
Lucilius, 18, 32, 33, 38

Macrobius, 68
Martial, 32, 58
Maximus of Tyre, 18, 26

Nicolaus of Myra, 29
Nøjgaard, M., 8f.

Ovid, 46, 63, 66, 70

Papyri
   PAmherst II.26, 29, 30, 37
   PBerol. inv. 11628, 75
   PGrenfell II.84, 29, 30, 37
   PColon. II.64, 37
   PMichigan 457, 29, 30, 37
   POxy. 1249, 3
   POxy. 1404, 29, 30, 37
   Papyrus Rylands 493, 23–25, 37, 44, 75, 89
   PSI 848, 37
Perotti, N., 3, 39
Perry, B. E., 6, 8
Petronius, 46, 76
Phaedrus, 3, 39–52
   Ademar Codex. See *Aesopus Latinus, Ademar Codex*
   Appendix Perottina, 3, 39f., 45, 51, 95

book structure, 40f., 51, 85
   Codex Pithoeanus, 39, 40, 45, 85, 95
   and Horace, 41f.
   language and style, 43f., 51, 75
   meter, 43f.
   moral criticism, 49f.
   prose paraphrases. *See Aesopus Latinus*
   self-reference, 41f., 50, 51
   sources, 44f., 51
   stele for tomb, 51f.
   textual history, 39f., 50
   topical allusions, 46–50, 51
   vita, 48, 51
Planudes, Maximus, 4, 73
Plato, 2, 12, 13, 17, 18, 19, 36
Plutarch, 17f., 26f., 59, 61
Pompeius Trogus, 17, 32
Ps.-Aphthonius, *Vita Aesopi,* 74
Ps.-Dositheus, 2, 30–31, 38, 53, 58, 59, 96, 102
Ps.-Lucian, *Lucius, or The Ass,* 18, 29
Ps.-Homer, *Margites,* 13, 18

Quintilian, 29, 32

Reiske, E., 7
Reiske, J. J., 7, 76
Rhetor Brancatianus, 90
Rohde, E., 10
Romulus, Roman king, 98
"Romulus." *See Aesopus Latinus,* "Romulus"

Schneider, J. G. , 7
Sejanus, 48, 49
Semonides, 12, 16, 18, 52
Seneca (the Younger), 32
"Seven Sages," 22, 26, 79
Simonides, 13, 17
Socrates, 18, 26, 63, 79
Solon, 13, 17, 26
Sophocles, 12, 17, 19, 20
Stesichorus, 11
Syntipas, 90

Tabulae Assendelftianae, 29, 30, 37, 53
Themistius, 26
Theodosius II, Roman emperor, 69
Theognis, 13, 17
Theon of Alexandria, 20, 29

Timocreon, 13, 17
Titianus, 64

Virgil, 67, 68
Vita Aesopi. See *Aesop Romance*

Xenophon, 12, 17, 18, 20, 59

Aesopica (ed. Perry)
74–77: 85
91: 55
105–109: 86
116: 86, 91
121: 92
155: 9, 41, 47
Aesopus Latinus (ed. Thiele)
3: 103
8: 103
15: 47f., 102
17: 103f.
19: 100f.
29: 101
59: 104
60: 98
Aphthonius, *Progymnasmata*
1: 74
Archilochus
frag. 172–181 West: 14
frag. 185–187 West: 14
Aristophanes
Aves 471: 12, 19, 29
Vespae 1401: 12, 15, 19
——— 1427–32: 12, 19, 21
——— 1435–40: 12, 19, 20
Aristotle, *Rhetorica* 1393a23–94a18:
11f., 23, 24
Ausonius, *Epistulae* 16.2.74–8: 64,
98
Avianus
3: 65–67
14: 71
20: 71
21: 71

37: 71
epistula: 63–65, 68f.
Babrius
1. *prol.*: 14, 52f., 59, 60
2. *prol.*: 54, 59, 60
31: 58
39: 55
40: 55, 58
57: 60
78: 62
88: 62
89: 9, 47, 62
95: 9, 58
100: 62
102: 61
109: 58, 65f., 67
129: 55–57
134: 61

Callimachus
Iambi 2: 52
Iambi 4: 36, 52

Ennius, *Saturae* frag. 21–58 Vahlen:
33, 38

Gellius, Aulus, *Noctes Atticae*
2.29.3–16: 33

Herodotus
1.141: 2, 12, 17, 36
2.134–135: 15
Hesiod, *Opera et dies* 202–212: 12,
13, 16, 17, 21, 36

Horace
  Epistulae 1.3.19–20: 2, 32, 34
  Sermones 2.3.312–320: 32, 34f.
  Sermones 2.6.79–117: 2, 32, 35, 47

Livy, *Ab urbe condita* 2.32.5–12: 17,
  31f., 38
Lucian
  Hermotimus 20: 28
  Piscator 36: 28
Lucilius, *Saturae* frag. 1074–81
  Krenkel: 32, 33, 38

Phaedrus
  1. *prol.*: 40, 41
  1.1: 9, 47, 49, 51, 103
  1.2: 41, 51
  1.5: 51
  1.13: 42–44, 55, 100f.
  1.15: 51
  1.29: 51
  1.30: 40f.
  2.6: 103

3. *prol.*: 16, 41f., 48, 49
3.7: 51, 65
3.12: 51
4.26: 51
  Ademar Codex 13 (= 15 Th.): 47f.,
    51
  Appendix Perottina 15: 45f., 51
Plato, *Alcibiades* (1) 123A: 2, 13, 36

Quintilian, *Institutio oratoria*
  5.11.19: 32

Scolion 9, frag. 892 Page: 12, 21

Theon, *Progymnasmata* 3: 20

Vita Aesopi
  100: 74, 83
  101–123: 14f., 78, 79, 84
  109–110: 84
  128: 82, 91
  129: 46
  131: 91

Niklas Holzberg

is Professor of Classics at the
University of Munich. He is
a renowned authority on
classical literature and has
published extensively on
ancient fiction, Roman elegy,
and the Aesop tradition.

Christine
Jackson-Holzberg

is translator of *The Ancient
Novel: An Introduction*, also
by Niklas Holzberg.

3 3295 00133 6608

PA 3032 .H65 2002
Holzberg, Niklas.
The ancient fable